RAF
TRAINING COMMAND

A PICTORIAL HISTORY

KEITH WILSON

PER LABOREM AD SUMMA

AMBERLEY

Acknowledgements

A project of this nature requires the help and support of many people, who have contributed in different ways to make the book possible. The author would like to offer his sincere thanks to the following:

Sebastian Cox at the Air Historical Branch, RAF Northolt, for providing the Branch's support with access to the collection of images and information, along with his encouragement and sense of humour.

My thanks must also go to Lee Barton at the Air Historical Branch for his unwavering enthusiasm, vision, and attention to detail during the image selection process. Also, thanks must go to his research skills, unearthing new information and responding to the never-ending stream of questions.

At Amberley Publishing I would like to thank Kevin Paul, Fraser Searle and Aaron Phull for their considerable input at key stages during the book's production.

Sincere thanks are due to my sons Sam and Oliver. Thank you for your patience and support throughout the project; I could not have done it without you.

Finally, my special thanks must go to Carol – for being there to support me throughout the project.

First published 2022

Amberley Publishing
The Hill, Stroud
Gloucestershire, GL5 4EP

www.amberley-books.com

Copyright © Keith Wilson, 2022

The right of Keith Wilson to be identified as the Author of this work has been asserted in accordance with the Copyrights, Designs and Patents Act 1988.

ISBN: 978 1 4456 6600 6 (print)
ISBN: 978 1 4456 6601 3 (ebook)

British Library Cataloguing in Publication Data.
A catalogue record for this book is available from the British Library.

Typeset in 10pt on 12.5pt Celeste.
Typesetting by SJmagic DESIGN SERVICES, India.
Printed in UK.

Contents

Introduction

Training aircraft of 12 Flying Training School in a hangar at Spittlegate, near Grantham, Lincolnshire, in April 1917. To the left of the image is serial number A1688, a Graeme White Type XV, powered by an 80hp Gnome engine. (*Crown Copyright/Air Historical Branch image H-2378*)

Terra caeloque docemus – 'We teach on land and in the air'

The Royal Air Force was planned in 1919 to have as its primary function the capacity to expand without drastic alteration. In Lord Trenchard's *Memorandum on the Permanent Organisation of the Royal Air Force in 1919*, he stated, 'The present need is … first and foremost, the making of a sound framework on which to build a service, which while giving us now the few essential service squadrons, will be capable of producing whatever time may show to be necessary in the future.'

Within this framework Lord Trenchard considered training to be of extreme importance. The capacity to expand depended on three main elements: an operational pattern on which to model the enlarged first line; a pursuit of technical development to equip it efficiently; and a study of the training required to correctly man it. Lord Trenchard went on to describe training as 'that on which the whole future of the Royal Air Force depends'.

Central Flying School (CFS)

Established at RAF Upavon, Wiltshire, on 12 May 1912, the Central Flying School was the military's primary institution for the training of military flying instructors. On 1 April 1918, the Royal Flying Corps (RFC) and Royal Naval Air Services (RNAS) were amalgamated to form the Royal Air Force. In 1920, as part of the reorganisation, the CFS became the Flying Instructors School and conducted the work previously undertaken by the School of Special Flying at Gosport.

As a result of further reorganisation in 1926, the CFS relocated to RAF Wittering, Cambridgeshire. Around this time the Air Ministry decided that in between courses the staff should visit the flying training schools to check whether the system and standard of instruction was being maintained. Effectively, this was the beginning of the Examining Wing.

In 1929, staff instructors from the CFS flew the Supermarine S.6 at Calshot, winning the Schneider Trophy for Great Britain. The S.6 was designed by R. J. Mitchell and in 1929 was powered by the then new 1,900hp Rolls-Royce R engine. It was an unbeatable combination. Two years later, flying the uprated and improved S.6B variant, the aircraft was once again victorious at Calshot enabling Great Britain to retain the trophy for all time. During this period, a certain Pilot Officer Frank Whittle, while serving at the CFS, patented the first jet engine.

Trenchard's Vision Does Not Become Reality

Sadly, from 1919 through to 1934, Trenchard's vision for training in the RAF did not become a reality. While it occupied a great deal of the RAF's time, training passed more and more into the background; the process of instruction became a settled, regular, familiar routine. During this period, there was little technical development requiring a reassessment of the training regime. Military aircraft in 1934 were much the same as those had been at the end of the First World War in 1918.

Furthermore, pressure on the British economy kept military expenditure down, which in turn meant the RAF's expenditure on flying schools and training was to be at an absolute minimum. Though a few essential teaching and training establishments had opened during the 1920s, by the following decade there was nothing to spare for more than the indispensable ancillaries to a small number of squadrons. Training had become less of a primary activity for schools while more of a secondary activity for squadrons – an inevitable result of the economy.

The squadrons had aircraft and experienced crews, so training was an obvious way of keeping them fully occupied. That said, employing squadrons on training had clear disadvantages too. Most squadrons were never particularly efficient because they always had a large proportion of pilots undergoing training, while this training was not undertaken by specialist instructors but by experienced pilots on whom the first line of defence depended. Since training was not the squadron's raison d'être it was sometimes treated with a lack of application and seriousness that often accompanied a minor role.

Clouds of War on the Horizon

By 1934 the international situation had deteriorated to such an extent that British Prime Minister Ramsay McDonald announced a new expansion programme for the Services. The CFS was again enlarged and became a unit within Flying Training Command and moved back to RAF Upavon in 1935.

The prestige of the RAF pilot training remained high, while the CFS maintained flying instruction at an admirable and polished standard. Training was excellent – but only within very narrow parameters. It was almost solely about producing pilots, was focussed upon short-range flying, and largely preoccupied with piloting ability. It had, in fact, become rather static and stereotyped in the form prescribed by the lessons of the First World War.

Unfortunately, there was a constant temptation to take the entire training process for granted. It was assumed the established order of training was entirely adequate to meet any demands that may be made upon it, while assuming the training element in the framework of expansion would inevitably be capable of producing whatever time might show to be necessary.

Expansion Plans

When the expansion of the RAF began in 1934, Air Commodore Tedder observed that the established order of school training not only failed to produce operational competence, but left so much to be done by the operational squadrons that they could only attain passable military efficiency after an uphill struggle. Some squadrons with more complicated roles never really succeeded in the struggle.

Pedder proposed to raise the standards of school instruction so that pilots would leave the facility as operationally competent pilots, although it would mean lengthening the period of instruction as well as revising the syllabus; despite the fact that the economic situation, combined with the expediency relating to the situation in Europe, compelled the time required to train a pilot to be reduced. Sadly, the reduction in time roughly offset the improvement in syllabus, so schools turned out new pilots at much the same established order, standard and rate.

Aside from the economy of cost, which was still a major consideration, the main obstacle preventing the raising of school standards was difficulty in providing instructors. The expansion programme demanded a larger flow of pilots, but to provide them with longer programmes would require a considerable increase in the number of schools. The existing RAF could not supply the instructors required for the new schools without seriously depleting the front line. It was preferred to keep the school training virtually unchanged rather than weaken the first line, even temporarily.

Unfortunately, this logistical problem would not go away and was still evident in both 1935 and 1936. So bad was the problem that it prevented the opening of specialised schools to deal with the training consequences of new technical developments.

As long-range, high-speed monoplanes entered service the training required became ever more complex. The size of the crews increased and now each crew member required thorough and specialised training. Accurate navigation became an urgent problem, as did the manning of the turrets and radar positions, while the greater all-weather day and night capabilities of aircraft required a significantly higher standard of day and night instrument flying.

Formation of RAF Training Command

It was against this somewhat sorry background of training and logistical problems, as well as having the clouds of war firmly visible on the horizon, that the decision was taken to form a new RAF Training Command on 1 May 1936, an organisation derived from the ashes of the former RAF Inland Area.

This book will tell the story – in words and pictures – of RAF Training Command from 1 May 1936 until it was separated into Flying Training Command and Technical Training Command on 27 May 1940. Both commands were absorbed into the newly re-established RAF Training Command on 1 June 1968, where it remained until being absorbed into RAF Support Command on 13 June 1977.

What is Included in this Volume?

The history of Flying Training within the RAF is a very substantial subject; far too large to be condensed into a volume of this size. Therefore, I have had to limit the subjects specifically to those activities conducted within RAF Training and Flying Training Commands. I have included details and images of some of the more interesting units and facilities that Training Command have controlled during those years, although this volume does place its emphasis on the activities of the Flying Training Schools.

Additional and specialist training was, and in many cases still is, conducted at the various Operational Conversion Units (OCUs) that exist, but these are more usually located at squadron levels while under the control of different Command structures. Over the years, many of these OCUs have featured interesting aircraft and activities, but nevertheless due to a lack of space I have been forced to excluded them. Perhaps the subject may make a possible title for a future date?

Images

As the title suggests, this is predominately a picture-led volume. In selecting the images for this book, I have often been obliged to choose between quality and originality. I have gone to considerable lengths to include as many previously unpublished images as possible but there are only a finite number of images held within the excellent corridors of the Air Historical Branch library.

Where a poor-quality image has been used, it is because I decided the interest value of the subject matter has warranted the decision, making it a better choice than perhaps a familiar image that has previously been published elsewhere.

I have thoroughly enjoyed researching this volume, the sixth in the 'A Pictorial History' series for Amberley Publishing. I sincerely hope this pictorial history of RAF Training Command enlightens and, more importantly, entertains the reader.

Keith Wilson
Ramsey, Cambridgeshire

Staff and pupils of the first course to pass through the Central Flying School, held between 17 August and 19 December 1912. Seated in the front centre is Captain Godfrey M. Paine RN, the commandant and at the end of the second row is Major Hugh M. Trenchard. (*Crown Copyright/Air Historical Branch image CFS-1*)

The first aeroplane accident suffered by the Central Flying School occurred in September 1912 when Bristol Boxkite No. 408 crashed at Upavon with Assistant Paymaster G. S. Trewin RN at the controls. (*Crown Copyright/Air Historical Branch image CFS-7*)

A Royal Aircraft Factory BE.2 two-seater photographed in 1912. (*Crown Copyright/Air Historical Branch image H-2154*)

Training aircraft in use with the Central Flying School at Upavon in 1913. Included in the line-up are Avro 500s, a pair of BE.4s, Henri Farman, Short S.27 and two Maurice Farman S.7 Longhorns, with No. 411 nearest the camera. (*Crown Copyright/Air Historical Branch image CFS-8*)

A Royal Air Factory BE.2c photographed in 1918. (*Crown Copyright/Air Historical Branch image H-1803*)

An Airco DH.6 trainer C4548 pictured at Thetford in 1918. (*Crown Copyright/Air Historical Branch image H-1181/ACM J. M. Robb*)

An SE.5a, serial number C9051, at an unidentified location in 1918. (*Crown Copyright/Air Historical Branch image H-2426*)

Sopwith Snipe E6837 of 5 Flying Training School based at Shotwick in 1920. (Crown Copyright/ Air Historical Branch image H-674)

A student pilot checks the aircraft technical logbook of his Bristol F.2 Fighter with a member of the groundcrew before a cross-country flight from the RAF College Cranwell in 1923. (*Crown Copyright/ Air Historical Branch image H-1096*)

Flight Cadet (later Air Marshal) R. L. R. Atcherley brings his Bristol Fighter – F4502/B7 – in to land on the grass strip at RAF Cranwell, *c.* 1924. A line of Avro 504K trainers (including D8863/C3) can be seen behind. (*Crown Copyright/Air Historical Branch image H-1097*)

Avro 504K trainers and personnel of 'A' Flight lined up at the RAF College Cranwell in 1924. (*Crown Copyright/Air Historical Branch image H-1098*)

An Avro 504 of No. 2 Flying Training School at RAF Digby in 1924. (*Crown Copyright/Air Historical Branch image H-1632*)

A mechanic in conversation with a pilot who is about to get airborne in dual control Bristol Fighter F.2, F4751, of 5 Flying Training School based at Sealand in 1927. (*Crown Copyright/Air Historical Branch image H-676*)

Armstrong Whitworth Atlas TM J9472 pictured in 1929 while serving with 1 Flying Training School based at Netheravon, Wiltshire. (*Crown Copyright/Air Historical Branch image H-703*)

Armstrong Whitworth Siskin IIIDC, J9219/3, of 3 Flying Training School based at RAF Spitalgate in 1929. (*Crown Copyright/Air Historical Branch image H-961*)

Three de Havilland Genet Moth trainer aircraft of the Central Flying School (CFS) photographed while performing at Hendon on 13 July 1929. (*Crown Copyright/Air Historical Branch image H-103*)

Established by the CFS at Little Rissington in 1972, the 'Vintage Pair' became a popular participant at airshows across the UK. Initial equipment was Vampire T.11 XH304 flying alongside Meteor T.7 WF791. This image was taken during a photographic sortie on 27 September 1977. Sadly, XH304 was lost following a mid-air collision with Meteor WA669 in 1986. (*Crown Copyright/Air Historical Branch image TN-1-7761*)

Formation of RAF Training Command (1 May 1936)

In the late 1920s, the Air Ministry began to consider a replacement RAF Trainer to replace the Avro 505N. The Hawker Tomtit first appeared in 1928 and was one of two types considered for small-scale production. Between 1928 and 1931, twenty-five aircraft were produced for the RAF operated with No. 3 Flying Training School (3FTS). The type remained in service until 1935 when all were retired and put up for sale. K1786 was sold onto the civilian market as G-AFTA and is now owned and operated by the Shuttleworth Trust at Old Warden, where it regularly appears in its former RAF training colours. (*Keith Wilson/SFB Photographic image 1-0199*)

The roots and requirements of a suitable training arm and a hurried pre-war expansion programme for the RAF can be traced back to the failures of the Geneva Disarmament Conference held in 1932–33. While this chapter is not a history of the Conference, it is beyond question that the interlude of two years profoundly affected the UK's subsequent attempt to build up an air strength to a level that could counter that of Germany's.

The Conference for the Reduction and Limitations of Armaments of 1932–34 (also known as the World Disarmament Conference or the Geneva Disarmament Conference) was a failed attempt by thirty-one member states of the League of Nations, together with the United States, to achieve disarmament. The Conference was held in Geneva from 1932 to 1934.

A preparatory commission was initiated by the League of Nations in 1925 and it seemed that, by 1931, there was sufficient support to hold a conference. This was duly opened under the chairmanship of former British Foreign Secretary Arthur Henderson and a message received from US President Franklin Roosevelt summed up the expectations of the conference when he said, 'If all nations will agree wholly to eliminate from possession and use the weapons which make a successful attack, defences automatically will become impregnable and the frontiers and independence of every nation will become secure.'

The talks were beset with difficulties from the outset. Germany, represented by Adolf Hitler, immediately demanded to be allowed military equality or it would leave. The French were equally insistent that German military inferiority was their only assurance from a future conflict as serious as they had endured in the First World War.

The League's failure to ensure the success of the talks increased the likelihood of a second major European conflict. However, Britain and the US were not prepared to offer the additional security commitments that France requested in exchange for limitations of French armaments. After ten months of negotiations, France, Britain and Italy announced that Germany and other states disarmed in accordance with the Treaty of Versailles should be insured equality in a system that provided security to all nations. Furthermore, the various parties were unable to agree what constituted 'Offensive' and 'Defensive' weapons.

Perhaps not unsurprisingly, the talks broke down. Hitler withdrew Germany from both the Conference and the League of Nations on 14 October 1933. By 1934, despite the best efforts of many countries, the Conference was over without reaching a resolution. Sadly, the 1930s had proved to be far too self-interested an international period to accommodate multilateral action in favour of peace.

The Conference is generally perceived as being a failure mainly due to the withdrawal of Germany from the talks, and the onset of the Second World War just five years later.

Rearmament Schemes of 1934–39

Following the end of the First World War, and the subsequent rundown in military forces, the rearming modestly planned by the UK in 1923 was leisurely pursued until reduced almost to a crawl in 1931, before coming to a full stop in 1932. The Depression that began in 1929 had a profound effect on government spending. Meanwhile, Germany was building an illegal and illicit air force.

On 23 March 1932, the British Cabinet decided to abolish the 'Ten Year Rule' and in the Air Estimates for 1934, authorised an increase in spending on first-line strength, along with the implications for training and support organisations.

Around this time, the total strength of the RAF was stated to be '785 first-line aircraft'. A comparison with the French Air Force can be made here, as their sated strength was more than 1,400 while it should be noted that Germany was seeking parity with France, which was significantly better equipped than the RAF.

The following years saw changes to Armament Groups and Armament Training Squadrons, along with new Gunnery Co-operation Flights and Torpedo Training Flights. In 1935, the Air Pilotage School at Andover became the Air Navigation School while three Coastal Defence Training Units were combined at Gosport as the Coast Defence Development Unit.

Old-fashioned Equipment

Equipment in use with the training establishments at the time were primarily based on designs from the 1920s such as the Sopwith Snipe, Avro Tutor, Hawker Tomtit and Fairey IIIF. That said, the first-line squadrons were primarily equipped with biplane fighters like the Hawker Hart, Fury I and II, Demon and Hind, although the monoplane Hurricane and Spitfire designs were clearly visible on the horizon.

Another steep change was heading for the training establishments. Newer, modern, more complex designs – especially in the case of multi-engine bombers – required a variety of different aircrew including a navigator, bomb aimer, wireless operator, and air gunners. All these unique trades would require their own specialist training to become effective and efficient crews.

However, Air Commodore Tedder observed that the establishment order of school training not only failed to produce operational competence, but left far too much to be completed by the operational squadrons – a major distraction from their intended (and required) roles, which were clearly diluting their efficiencies. Pedder proposed to raise the standard of school instruction so that pilots would leave the initial training facilities as operationally competent pilots, thereby relieving the first-line squadrons of these onerous tasks. It would mean increasing the period of training required on the revised courses and revising considerably the syllabus under which this training was conducted. Unfortunately, the economic situation required the time to train operationally ready pilots to be reduced, so the new syllabus was completed in a shorter time, thereby producing new pilots at a similar established order and rate.

New Elementary and Reserve Training Schools

One significant change was the decision taken by the Director of Training that civilian-run primary training schools would take over the responsibility for initial pilot training, thereby leaving the Flying Training Schools (FTSs) free to continue with the more advanced training – particularly on the newer types of aircraft now entering first-line squadrons – and relieving operational squadrons of providing what was effectively a training 'finishing school'.

The new schools were called Elementary and Reserve Flying Training Schools (E&RFTSs), with the first four being formed in the summer of 1935 and had, in fact, been in operation since 1923–23 involved in the training of reservists. However, within the next four years, a further fifty-nine such schools had been created or were planned at civilian airfields across the UK.

While this expansion programme was underway, three University Air Squadrons (UASs) were providing flying instruction to undergraduates from the major universities: the Cambridge UAS had formed in October 1925 and began flying on Avro Tutor aircraft at Duxford in May 1926; the Oxford UAS formed in October 1925 and began flying in January 1928 at Upper Heyford on the Avro Tutor; while the London UAS was formed in October 1935 and began flying shortly afterwards at Northolt, once again on the Avro Tutor.

By 1936, with the political situation in Europe steadily worsening, the RAF was beginning to receive better, although more complex, equipment, with anything other than the single-seat aircraft requiring the addition of two or more crew members now requiring a pilot and an observer or bomb aimer. Others, including the coastal aircraft required multi-skilled crew members while some bombers now required two pilots. To address this problem, the specialist training schools that had effectively disappeared in 1919 at the conclusion of the First World War would have to be set up and modernised. The first was the Air Observers School at North Coates in 1936 on Gordon and Wallace aircraft. The problem of suitable navigation training was resolved by combining the Air Navigation School at Andover with the Navigation School at Calshot to form a new School of Air Navigation at Manston equipped with Avro Anson aircraft. These were later joined by the Saro Cloud aircraft of the Seaplane Training Squadron.

Time for a Significant Structural Change

Meanwhile, the number of E&RFTSs had increased to thirteen, meeting the initial objectives set by the authorities, while the number of FTSs was also increasing. However, the entire RAF administrative structure was coming under increasing pressure to cope and a major structural change was required – and it was not just within the training regime, as a major devolution was overdue.

Consequently, it was decided that the Air Ministry would in future only be responsible for policy-making decisions, and its instructions would be carried out through a chain structure, starting with Commands and progressing downwards through Groups, Stations and Units. The then existing Area Commands would cease to exist, to be replaced by specialised Bomber, Coastal, Fighter, and Training Commands. On 1 May 1936 Training Command was created, having been formed from the Inland Area, while 23 Group was restyled No. 23 (Training) Group.

Further reorganisation took place in July when the control of all technical training units became the responsibility of No. 24 (Training) Group at Halton.

As Bentley Priory was now required as the headquarters of the new Fighter Command, Training Command headquarters was moved to Buntingsdale Hall, near Market Drayton on 13 July. While on paper the RAF now had an improved training structure, it took the new Command some time to settle into its task.

Expansion Under Way

A further twenty reserve schools had been authorised, with the first coming into operation in July 1937 at Castle Bromwich, Redhill and Shoreham. Interestingly, Advanced Flying Training had been added to their syllabus while their fleets of Tiger Moth and Magister aircraft were being supplemented by Hart Trainer, Fairey Battle and Avro Anson aircraft. With the number of ERFTSs continuing to increase, the task of managing them was handed to a new No. 26 (Training) Group, formed at Hendon on 1 December 1937.

A Year of Many Changes

1938 was a year of considerable change within Training Command – some purely involving name changes, while others meant new specialist units. A School of General Reconnaissance opened at Thorney Island, while a Floatplane Training School formed at Calshot in April. Many new E&RFTSs appeared during the year, while some now, which had an Anson on strength for navigation training, saw these break away to form new (and separate) Civil Air Navigation Schools (CANS). The first four were based at Prestwick (No. 1), Yatesbury (No. 2), Desford (No. 3) and Ansty (No. 4). Another five CANS units were created in the following year.

On 1 November 1938 a new Balloon Command was formed for controlling the numerous barrage balloon units likely to be required on the outbreak of hostilities. Nos 30 to 33 (Barrage Balloon) Groups were founded, followed by No. 34 in April 1940.

During 1939, the expansion continued apace with increases in both FTSEs and CANSs, while No. 21 (Training) Group was formed at Cranwell to take on responsibility for the base along with the RAF College. Another change becoming apparent was the increased use of monoplanes at many training establishments with the issue of twin-engine Airspeed Oxford aircraft, alongside the single-engine North American Harvard I and home-produced Miles Master I aircraft.

The scene was set for the outbreak of the Second World War, but even the new structure and equipment would not provide sufficient aircrew from within the facilities based in the UK. Assistance with RAF training would be required elsewhere.

Britain entered the Second World War with a front-line strength with an optimistic estimate of around 50 per cent of that of Germany, although in reality it may have even been significantly less than that. In a speech by Lord Beaverbrook, then Lord Privy Seal and formerly Minister of Aircraft Production, to the House of Lords on 19 January 1941, he gave the first-line strength of Germany at the beginning of the war as 4,320 aircraft, further stating that it was 'four-times the strength of Britain's', meaning that Britain's was around just 1,100 aircraft.

The Avro 504N was designed as a replacement for the wartime 504K and became the first new trainer adopted by the RAF after the First World War. It provided excellent service at Flying Training Schools, as well as University Air Squadrons, before being superseded by the Avro Tutor, beginning in 1932. This image shows Avro 504N, J8504, of 601 Squadron pictured at Hendon in 1929. (Crown *Copyright/Air Historical Branch image H-37*)

A dual control Fairey IIIF Mk IIIB (DC), S1847/H, of 'C' Flight at the RAF Training Base at Leuchars around 1934. (*Crown Copyright/Air Historical Branch image H-1843*)

Hawker Tomtit I, K1451, of No. 3 Flying Training School based at Grantham in the early 1930s. This aircraft had been delivered to the FTS in November 1930 where it remained until retired in February 1935. It was later sold and became G-AEVO in April 1937. (*Crown Copyright/Air Historical Branch image H-649*)

Avro Tutor K3263/3 of No. 5 Flying Training School after it had run into K3251 at RAF Sealand on 29 October 1934. The aircraft was repaired and returned to service, initially with 1 FTS and later the RAF College, before suffering another landing accident on 23 April 1936. It was again repaired and continued in service with the RAF College until August 1938, when it was struck off charge. (*Crown Copyright/Air Historical Branch image H-2231*)

Bristol Bulldog, K2188, was initially manufactured as a single-seat aircraft but was later converted as the first two-seat 'TM' trainer. The aircraft was delivered to the Aeroplane and Armament Experimental Establishment at Boscombe Down on 30 December 1931 for handling trials. In March 1935, the aircraft was transferred to the Central Flying School for evaluation before being returned to its manufacturer to allow the installation of a Cheetah engine. Between December 1935 and May 1940, the aircraft was used for a series of engine trials at the Royal Aircraft Establishment at Farnborough before being retired and relegated to instructional duties in May 1940. (*Crown Copyright/ Air Historical Branch image H-1563*)

Probably one of the world's best-known training aircraft, the de Havilland Tiger Moth was first introduced into RAF service in 1932, where it remained for the next fifteen years as a standard elementary training aircraft with Flying Training Command until 1947, and until 1951 with the RAF Volunteer Reserve, becoming the RAF's very last biplane training aircraft. R-5136 was originally built with construction number 83018, part of a batch of 400 aircraft ordered at the outbreak of the Second World War. It joined the RAF in 1940 where it remained until withdrawn from service in 1957. It was sold onto the civilian marketplace and registered as G-APAP before being converted into a Thruxton Jackaroo. However, it was later converted back into a Tiger Moth and repainted into its former RAF colours as 'R-5136'. It was photographed during a sortie from Henlow on 23 September 2003. (*Keith Wilson/SFB Photographic image 1-0117*)

Hawker Hart Trainer, K5892, in service with 10 Flying Training School at Ternhill in 1937. The aircraft joined No. 7 Flying Training School in July 1939 and was later damaged in a crosswind landing at RAF Netheravon in April 1940 and struck-off charge. (*Crown Copyright/Air Historical Branch image H-219*)

Fitters at work in the Engine Repair Section at No. 6 Flying Training School, RAF Netheravon, on 3 June 1937. (*Crown Copyright/Air Historical Branch image AHB-GSR-8174*)

The first production Avro Anson I made its initial flight in December 1935 and entered RAF service with Flying Training Command the following year. K8828 was delivered to No. 1 Air Observers School in July 1937 before being transferred to the No. 2 School of Navigation in 1939. It remained in service until struck-off charge in September 1943. This image depicts K8828 at RAF North Coates while the aircraft was in service with No. 1 Air Observers School. (*Crown Copyright/Air Historical Branch image CH-138*)

The Airspeed Oxford was one of the new types ordered for the RAF expansion programme. When the type entered service with the Central Flying School in November 1937, it became the RAF's first twin-engine monoplane advanced trainer. This image shows three Airspeed Oxford Is (N4640, P6823/24 and N6259) of No. 14 Service Flying Training School based at Cranfield, Bedfordshire, flying in formation over the local countryside in August 1940. (*Crown Copyright/Air Historical Branch image CH-1097*)

The Hawker Hind Trainer was a two-seat dual-control variant of the Hind light bomber, which superseded the Hart Trainer. The RAF took delivery of a total of 164, including 139 converted from the light-bomber version. K5401 was photographed at RAF Wyton in March 1937 when the aircraft was in service with 44 Squadron. In July 1938, it was transferred to 611 Squadron and then the RAF College in September 1939 before being struck-off charge in October 1940. (*Crown Copyright/Air Historical Branch image H-975*)

The Miles Magister was the first monoplane trainer to be used by the RAF on its introduction to service in September 1937, when L5913 was delivered to the Central Flying School. N3788 was built in 1941 and remained in service with several Elementary Flying Schools until withdrawn in 1948. It was transferred to the civil register as G-AKPF, where it has remained. The aircraft was restored to its former RAF training colours as N3788 and was photographed during a sortie from Old Warden on 25 July 2012. (*Keith Wilson/SFB Photographic image 2-0102*)

The North American Harvard was first delivered to the RAF in December 1938 and remained standard equipment of Flying Training Schools for more than sixteen years. The Harvard 1 was the British version of the US Army Air Corps (USAAC) BC-1 and the RAF received a total of 400 of this variant. Harvard I, N7033, of No. 2 Service Flying Training School, RAF Brize Norton, was photographed in flight with undercarriage lowered in July 1940. (*Crown Copyright/Air Historical Branch image CH-606*)

The prototype Miles Master (N3300) made its first flight in 1938 with the first deliveries being made to the RAF in May 1938, just ahead of the outbreak of the Second World War. Eventually, production reached a total of 900 aircraft. Miles Master 1s were used by Flying Training Schools at Sealand, Montrose and Hullavington. This image shows Miles Master I, N7576/F, of No. 14 Service Flying Training School, parked with other training aircraft on the hardstanding at Cranfield, in the summer of 1940. (*Crown Copyright/Air Historical Branch image CH-1089*)

Flying Training Command During the Second World War (1939–45)

The de Havilland Tiger Moth was first introduced into RAF service in February 1932 and served for the next fifteen years. During the Second World War, most RAF pilots were trained on the Tiger Moth. British production reached 4,668 examples for the RAF while a further 2,751 were built in Canada, Australia, and New Zealand for the Commonwealth Training Plan. After the war, large numbers of Tiger Moth aircraft were disposed of onto the civilian market and gained something of a cult following. As a result, many airframes are still flying today including these two examples – G-ADWJ flying as BB803/75 and G-ALWS flying as N-9328/69 – both of which were beautifully restored into their original RAF colours by Kevin Crumplin. They were photographed in November 2014 when both aircraft featured the foldaway blind-flying hood fitted over the rear cockpit. (*Keith Wilson/SFB Photographic image 3-2174*)

On 1 September 1939, Hitler invaded Poland from the west. Just two days later, France and the UK declared war on Germany, beginning the Second World War. The declaration led to an immediate rationalisation of the training structure.

The Reserve aspect of the E&FTS was dropped overnight; all those schools not actually in full operation were closed. The remainder were drastically pruned in number and brought into the mainstream RAF as Elementary Flying Training Schools (EFTSs), though continuing to be operated by civilian organisations. As before, successful pupils would continue to move on to the Flying Training Schools, although they were renamed as Service Flying Training Schools (SFTSs). These included four FTS in Egypt, which moved to Habbaniya, Iraq, as four SFTS. Several other UK-based units were moved to make way for operational squadrons, especially in the south and east coast aerodromes, which were now required for defensive duties by operational front-line squadrons.

At the outbreak of the Second World War, the standard of both navigation and air gunnery training left a lot to be desired. In an attempt to remedy this, the pre-war civilian-operated Civil Air Navigation Schools (CANSs) were subsequently transferred into Air Observer and

Navigation Schools, while their instructors were mobilised into the RAF. At the same time, the navigation training task was withdrawn from existing regular units and several of the observer schools were then utilised as the basis for new Bombing and Air Gunnery schools.

All About People

It must be considered that the system of recruiting young men for flying duties in the RAF was not, as the word may imply, a policy of press-ganging all and sundry, training them, and seating them in an aeroplane. It was a policy – a science, in fact – of selecting, from the widest possible field, the most suitable personnel for the task. In modern warfare (such as the Second World War), time is the important factor, and in a highly technical service calling for a high degree of skill from the personnel concerned, the length of time spent in training, though necessarily long, must be reduced to a minimum.

There were always sufficient volunteers available for aircrew duties, and, given enough time, most of these personnel could probably have been trained to operate in the air. In 1939, however, the RAF did not have sufficient time, nor for that matter enough money, to indulge in such luxuries. It was essential that only those personnel with the requisite medical and educational standards and possessed a keen desire to fly and fight in the air were selected for training as aircrew. The primary task for the Inspector of Recruiting and the Director of Manning was therefore to tap all sources of manpower and to ensure that a sufficient quantity of suitable personal were available at all times to fill all of the courses at the Flying Training Schools.

The recruiting field was extended to cover the whole British and Allied world, and the peacetime rule that only persons of unmixed European descent were eligible for RAF service was abolished. During the war there were few nations, colours, or creeds that were not represented in the RAF – the keenness of overseas recruits to serve with the RAF was self-evident. Individual instances of the urge to serve could be quoted at length, from the Anglo-American individual from Japan who did two hours dual flying in a Japanese flying school in order to strengthen his chances of joining the RAF, to the volunteer from Patagonia who travelled 800 miles by every known and unknown form of transport to reach his port of embarkation. Then there was a young volunteer from the Czech-Poldi Steel Works, Osaka, whose father was of Persian extraction, born in Hong Kong and whose mother was of Danish-American-Japanese parentage, who was somewhat relieved at the lifting of the 'unmixed European descent' ban!

Formation of Aircrew Selection Boards

Upon the outbreak of the Second World War, steps that had been planned under the War Training Organisation (WTO) were taken to accelerate the training process; course lengths were drastically reduced, schools expanded, and new units formed to ensure the smooth and rapid flow of candidates into the training organisations. The selection machinery was reorganised, and eight Aviation Candidate Selection Boards (ACSBs) were formed on 3 September 1939 to select and attest candidates for the four aircrew categories of pilot, observer, wireless operator/ air gunner, and air gunner. Medical Boards (AOMBs) were also established at all the selection boards to carry out a thorough medical examination of all candidates.

Personnel were recruited through combined recruiting centres that examined all personnel joining any branch of the armed forces, and those expressing a desire to serve as aircrew were forwarded to the RAF ACSBs via a receiving centre. These eight ACSBs were located at Uxbridge (four), Padgate (two) and Uxbridge (two). Each of these eight selection boards had a weekly capacity of 125 candidates, providing a maximum total throughput of 1,000 candidates per week.

Creation of Initial Training Wings and Receiving Wings

It was obvious that, while the pre-war method of training had been satisfactory – where leisurely training courses and squadron activities would permit adequate time being spent on all subjects while the cadet was at his Primary Training Squadron (PTS), and later while on his squadron – this system would not stand up to the rigours of training for war. The squadrons would be too busy with operational flying to conduct any training, while training schools would have to direct their undivided attention to the flying training of pupils. Some basic training in navigation, mathematics, airmanship, and other subjects that the pupil would need to undertake at his flying school, could just as easily be taught at non-flying establishments. This would also have the added advantage that all personnel arriving at a flying school would have a common minimum standard of education.

In addition, some form of pool would be required to ensure a smooth and steady flow of pupils passed into the flying schools. Moreover, with an obvious need to widen the field of selection of aircrew candidates, eventually it became necessary to raise the educational levels of otherwise suitable raw material, a consideration that became increasingly important as the war progressed.

During the war the ground training organisation for aircrew personnel developed from the two-week disciplinary training course at Uxbridge to a series of courses lasting, in some cases, up to six months. The three main developments in this organisation, under the control of No. 54 Group, were:

1. The Preliminary Aircrew Training Scheme (PATS)
2. The Aircrew Reception Centre (ACRC)
3. The Initial Training Wings (ITW)

These did not develop in this order; in fact, the ITWs were the first to form, followed by the ACRCs, while the PATS scheme did not fully develop until 1943.

Shortly before the outbreak of war it had been planned, under the WTO, to set up ITWs to provide a thorough grounding in discipline and elementary instruction in ground subjects for aircrew candidates. The course, which was to be the first stage in the career of aircrew pupils, was to last a month, after which personnel were to be selected for training as pilots, observers, or air gunners. It was intended in 1939 that two such schools, each with a capacity for 350 pupils, should be formed within seven days of the outbreak of war.

In the early months the ITWs were crowded, and the period pupils stayed in them was longer than planned due to the restricted intake of flying training. By February 1940, there were over 2,500 pupils in the ITWs awaiting entry into the flying training schools – almost six months' supply – and it seemed possible that men may have to remain in ITWs for as long as seven to eight months. Unfortunately, the flow through EFTSs and AONs could not immediately be speeded up, and neither the number nor the capacity of SFT could be increased.

Eventually, by May 1940, the flow from the LTWs was quickened by starting advanced elementary flying courses, increasing EFTS capacity, and shortening the EFTS and SFT courses.

Recruiting in the Dominions and the Empire Training Plan

Despite the rush of volunteers and the measures taken to accept as many as possible, first-line squadrons were desperately short of trained aircrew personnel. For the first two years of the war, in fact, while the training machine was in process of expanding, demand far outstripped supply. Although courses were drastically curtailed, it still took many months to train a pilot and observer for operational duties. The reserve and auxiliary forces provided a substantial number of trained or partially trained personnel during the opening months of the war but few of the RAFVR personnel were trained up to a standard enabling them to take their place immediately in the front line; the large majority were in various stages of their training, thus enabling a pool of suitable volunteers to be established.

Nevertheless, the shortage of experienced personnel persisted, and steps had to be taken to widen the field of recruiting to the colonies and foreign countries where suitable personnel were likely to be available. Consequently, during the course of the war, about 4,200 candidates from every part of the world joined the RAF.

In the Dominions of Canada, Australia and New Zealand the vast Empire Air Training Scheme was launched, which was designed to recruit a total of 32,300 candidates per year. It was estimated, after allowing for training wastage and rejects, the scheme would provide 28,300 basically trained aircrew per year for service with the RAF. The Empire Training Schemes will be considered in more detail within Chapter 3 (see pages 39 to 50).

A Step-change in Throughput

In 1934, the RAF trained around 300 new pilots; by the end of 1941, the annual rate of output throughout the Empire was 22,000. In the same seven years the number of non-pilot aircrew rose from none in 1934 to 18,000 in 1941. The pre-war needs of the RAF in terms of personnel, and the problem of recruiting sufficiently suitable personnel for flying, were always forthcoming – mainly through the short-service commission scheme. The problem resolved itself merely into the selection and training of these personnel. In peacetime, the process was a simple one, but in times of war it became a far more complicated one.

Organisational and Structural Changes in Training Command

The rapid increase in training units was proving too great for the existing administration, and on 27 May 1940 Training Command was split into Flying Training Command and Technical Training Command. The former comprised numbers 21 and 23 Groups managing advanced flying training, while 51 Group controlled the elementary training units, and 54 Group was responsible for recruits.

By 1942, advanced flying training and crew training was largely being provided by the Dominion schools, which considerably relieved the burden on home-based units, although it did provide a rather fluctuating supply of men who had conducted their training in conditions vastly different from the European Theatre. To counter this problem the surviving UK-based SFTSs were restyled as (Pilot) Advanced Flying Units, with the primary task of getting Dominion trained pilots used to the vagaries of the British weather and terrain, along with blackout conditions.

The scope of the Operational Training Units (OTUs) was increased in 1943 with the formation of the first Transport OTUs. Initially equipped with Wellington aircraft, as the supply of US-built Dakota aircraft increased they switched to the new type. Crews were able to practice the kind of flying that would be required of them once they reached an airborne transport or glider towing squadron. These units were all eventually upgraded to Conversion Units specialising in different aspects of the transport role, with later equipment including Halifax and York transport aircraft.

The End of the Second World War

By the end of 1944 the Commonwealth scheme had largely served its purpose and was beginning to run down, and their duties returned to the UK. With the looming prospect of victory in Europe, preparations began for the war in the Far East. Emphasis was placed on tactical training and many bomber OCUs were replaced with similar units specialising in various transport conversion roles in preparation for the battles that were thought to lie ahead in the Far East.

All this proved unnecessary with the dropping of the first two atomic weapons by the United States in August 1945 – on Hiroshima and Nagasaki – and the eventual capitulation of Japan.

This image, taken on 4 September 1940, depicts Miles Magister, G-AFBS/A, of 8 Elementary Flying Training School, based at RAF Woodley, in flight with the blind-flying hood unfolded over the pupil's cockpit. This aircraft was impressed from the civilian register and was subsequently given the serial number BB661. In 1948, the aircraft returned to the British civil aircraft register as G-AFBS, being registered as a Miles M.14A Hawk Trainer 3. It served with Airways Aero Associated Limited and the Denham Flying School before eventually being permanently withdrawn from use. (*Crown Copyright/Air Historical Branch image CH-1255*)

Five Harvard I aircraft of No. 2 Service Flying Training School, lined up at RAF Brize Norton in July 1940. Nearest the camera is N7146, while P5894 and P5899 are also visible. (*Crown Copyright/ Air Historical Branch image CH-611*)

The wonderfully named Reid and Sigrist R.S.1 Snargasher, a twin-engine, three-seat advanced trainer that featured a sliding rear canopy for the three-seat configuration that was popular at the time. The prototype, registered G-AEOD, made its first flight in 1939. It was impressed into RAF use during wartime training and served at a variety of Elementary Training Schools. Further developments of the type were suspended as Reid and Siegrist became an important wartime manufacturer of instrumentation, as well as production subcontractors and repairers of the Boulton Paul Defiant and Hawker Hurricane assemblies. The R.S.1 was later used as a communications aircraft by the company until the prototype was broken up in 1944. (*Crown Copyright/Air Historical Branch image CH-2365*)

The Blackburn Botha was one of the new types of aircraft chosen for the re-equipment programme in Coastal Command, which was just about to commence when war broke out in 1939. However, the type was a failure within Coastal Command due to it being seriously underpowered, and was quickly transferred into operational training duties. This image depicts Blackburn Botha I, L6123/AQ, of 1 (Coastal) Operational Training Unit running up its engines at RAF Silloth in December 1940. (*Crown Copyright/Air Historical Branch image CH-1905*)

The Franco-Belgium Air Training School was formed at RAF Odiham on 28 October 1940 to train refugee pilots. Initially it was equipped with eighteen Magister I, four Morane 230 and three Caudron Simoun aircraft. The School was relatively short-lived, however, as it was disbanded on 9 June 1941. This image shows Free French trainee pilots prepare for take-off in Miles Magister I aircraft RAF Odiham. (*Crown Copyright/Air Historical Branch image CH-2054/LAC J. H. Adams*)

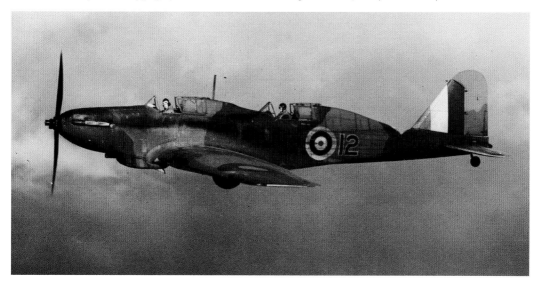

Although already considered obsolescent at the outbreak of the Second World War, there were around one thousand Fairey Battle aircraft in service with the RAF at the time. Another variant of the Fairey Battle bomber developed was this dual-control trainer version, designated the Fairy Battle T (for Trainer), with separate cockpits in place of the previous long canopy. Around two hundred were constructed and served with Nos 1, 7, 11 and 12 Flying Training Schools as well as around fifty aircraft sent to training schools in Canada. This image shows R7365/12 of No. 1 Flying Training School at RAF Netheravon. (*Crown Copyright/Air Historical Branch image CH-2140*)

Two Hotspur II gliders (BT551/L, nearest the camera) of No. 2 Glider Training Unit based at RAF Weston-on-the-Green, photographed in free flight over the Oxfordshire countryside during a training sortie on 27 June 1942. Originally conceived as an 'Assault' glider that necessitated a compact design allowing no more than eight troops being carried, later tactical philosophy favoured larger numbers of troops being carried into theatre aboard each glider, which meant the Hotspur gliders were relegated to training establishments where they became the basic training platforms for the glider schools that were formed. (*Crown Copyright/Air Historical Branch image CH-6030*)

A Miles Master II advanced trainer W8729/7, followed by an Airspeed Oxford, taxiing around the perimeter track to get into position for take-off at the Empire Central Flying School at RAF Hullavington in December 1942. This variant of the Master was powered by an 870hp Bristol Mercury XX radial engine. (*Crown Copyright/Air Historical Branch image CH-8194/LAC J. H. Adams*)

...whereas the earlier Miles Master I had been powered by the 715hp Rolls-Royce Kestrel XXX V-12 engine. This gave the aircraft an impressive performance with a top speed of close to 300mph. This image shows the first American volunteer pilots to serve with the RAF undergoing training at No. 5 Flying Training School at RAF Sealand, receiving instruction on the Miles Master I training aircraft in October 1940. Shortly after this image was taken No. 5 FTS moved to RAF Ternhill, taking its contingent of around 100 Miles Master I aircraft with it. (*Crown Copyright/Air Historical Branch image CH-1494*)

A trainee pilot and his instructor (in the front cockpit) preparing for a flight in a de Havilland Tiger Moth, serial T-5634/16, at No. 22 Elementary Flying Training School, Cambridge, in October 1942. (*Crown Copyright/Air Historical Branch image CH-7476*)

Miles Master III, W8825/43, of 5 (Pilots) Advanced Flying Unit ((P) AFU) based at RAF Ternhill was photographed in flight on 28 June 1942. This unit had been formed at Ternhill on 1 April 1942 and originated from No. 5 SFTS and led a somewhat nomadic life until disbanded on 21 June 1945. This image shows the instructor's screen (in the rear cockpit) to good effect. (*Crown Copyright/ Air Historical Branch image CH-6473*)

The de Havilland Mosquito T.3 was a two-seat dual-control trainer variant of the Mosquito. The prototype was converted from a NF.11 variant and made its first flight on 30 January 1942 and was soon delivered to the Mosquito Training Unit (later 1655 MTU) at Marham in September 1942. The T.3 variant continued in service with Flying Training Command right through the remainder of the Second World War. Post-war, the Mosquito T.3 equipped No. 204 Advanced Flying School at RAF Cottesmore and the type remained in service with OTUs until 1953. This example, RR299, was built at Leavesden in 1945 before serving in the Middle East. When its service career came to an end, it was acquired by Hawker Siddeley in 1963 and registered G-ASKH. It continued to operate on the flying display circuit until being destroyed in a fatal accident in July 1996. (*Keith Wilson/SFB Photographic*)

According to the original wartime caption: 'An entirely new system of the training of "night flyers" has been evolved following on experiments originating in the Spring of 1940, when night flying training in the RAF became a critical problem. Owing to enemy raids and the blackout, the night landing of RAF aircraft on illuminated airfields had to be abandoned and a new method was evolved from experiments carried out by Mr. C. H. Wood of Bradford, a technical photographic specialist in colour filters, and his brother, then Pilot Officer A. W. Wood, a Senior Link Trainer Instructor. Colour filters, as used in photography for adjusting contrasts, etc., cut out definite portions of the spectrum while transmitting others and, as the result of experiments, the Wood Brothers evolved a combination of light absorption filters which isolated the wavelength of monochromatic sodium light, which could thus remain visible through otherwise dark filters. They were successful in providing filters which excluded daylight but left all bright lights visible to form a flarepath, and its success at once opened the way to general night flying during day-time.' (*Crown Copyright/Air Historical Branch image CH-16859/LAC J. H. Adams*)

A graphic to explain how two pale coloured transparencies form a night effect. One is fitted to the aircraft windows and allows the instructors full external vision, while the other is worn as goggles by the pupils and limits his vision solely to the interior of the aircraft. (*Crown Copyright/Air Historical Branch image CH-16861/LAC J. H. Adams*)

The scientific principles involved were applied experimentally in a variety of ways – in goggles, in windows and in parts of goggles and windows. By filtering the daylight in two stages, i.e. one component part in the goggles and the other in an outer screen on the aircraft window, the two-stage system gave good vision of instruments without any cockpit lighting, but the single-stage method (all the filters in the form of goggles) obviated the need of coloured windows or hoods but necessitated the development of the sodium cockpit lighting. It is of special interest to note that the aircrews in training for the Mohne Dam raid were trained on the two-stage method – with instructors viewing through the pale coloured window. This image shows one of the later iterations of the light-tight goggles worn by the pupil, through which only sodium light is visible. (*Crown Copyright/Air Historical Branch image CH-16862/LAC J. H. Adams*)

This image, shot through the coloured goggles, demonstrates just how effective the goggles were at producing a night-time effect during daylight. (*Crown Copyright/ Air Historical Branch image CH-16864/ LAS J. H. Adams*)

The final piece of the jigsaw that enabled the daytime training of night flying was the incorporation of the sodium flare paths on runways. This image shows one of the sodium flare path lighting units being adjusted ahead of a night-flying training sortie during daylight. (*Crown Copyright/Air Historical Branch image CH-16865/LAC J. H. Adams*)

Wartime Overseas Training Programmes (1939–45)

Three Harvard aircraft of No. 2 Service Flying Training School at Uplands, Ontario, flying in formation above the snow-covered Canadian landscape in March 1943. These aircraft all carry RCAF markings with the first aircraft being serial number 2695 and the remaining two unidentified aircraft carrying the code letters 'II' and IW'. (*Crown Copyright/Air Historical Branch image CAN-2317*)

The concept of RAF training overseas was not a new one. The subject has a long history, having begun in 1915 during the First World War with training facilities and schemes in Canada, Australia and New Zealand, with several flying training schools opening near Fort Worth, Texas. South Africa also provided several pilots, but all of these were trained in the UK or the Middle East. Pilots from Canada, New Zealand, and South Africa served in the RFC, RNAS and the RAF.

The only RAF training unit stationed abroad on the outbreak of the Second World War was 4 FTS located at Au Sueir, Egypt, although proposals to establish flying training schools overseas had been made as far back as 1936.

Expansion Scheme 'F'

The first proposals for overseas training facilities were proposed by the pre-war RAF Expansion Scheme 'F', which brought the Director of Organisations in May 1936 to conclude that England would be very congested after Scheme 'F' had been completed. He suggested the congestion should be relieved by establishing overseas those units that would not necessarily be in the UK for strategic reasons.

Around this time three distinct conceptions for overseas training were germinating. The first was to locate RAF training schools overseas, as with 4 FTS at Abu Sueir. The second was a scheme for the Dominion training of Dominion recruits for service with the RAF, while the third was a plan for 'nominally Dominion but virtually British' schools training to RAF requirements. Although none of these schemes were proceeded with, they did have an influence in later developments.

India, New Zealand, Australia, South Africa, Palestine, Kenya, and Rhodesia were all considered as possible locations for RAF training schools. However, since the problem was not of overwhelming urgency, nothing was proceeded with. In July 1936, the RAF had eleven flying training schools at work in the UK, although five of these were located at aerodromes earmarked for operational purposes and all but one was due to relocate to a non-operational status within the following year or two. It was only a question of finding one suitable location, and there was plenty of time to do it – wasn't there?

Caithness and Northern Ireland were considered as possible locations – presumably, their remoteness caused them to be regarded as 'overseas' – but the prevalence of low cloud coupled with their geographical features was considered a major handicap.

Canada was still the main attraction, although there was political resistance. To make the idea of an RAF school in Canada more acceptable to the Canadian government, it was proposed that a school should be established in Canada that could be nominally Canadian, although its output would go directly to the RAF. However, the first of a series of official presentations to the Canadian government during the following three years, schemes – which eventually blossomed into the Empire Air Training Scheme – were not acceptable to the Canadian authorities who were sensitive about the views held by the French 'bloc'. In June 1937, the Air Ministry concluded that plans for the establishment of a flying training school in Canada could be regarded as dead.

Thankfully, this situation was resolved when Expansion Scheme 'L' was proposed in April 1938. Initially rejected by Prime Minister Mackenzie King in May 1938, the matter was overturned by the Canadian Parliament and a modified Scheme 'L' was eventually accepted in April 1939.

Rush of Volunteers When War Breaks Out

When war was finally declared on 3 September 1939, there was a rush of volunteers willing to sign up. Despite this, the first-line squadrons were short of suitably trained aircrew and this situation would continue for the first two years of the conflict.

However, the Empire Air Training Scheme was eventually launched, and the combined efforts of Australia, Canada, and New Zealand eventually provided a supply of 32,300 candidates per year, of which it was estimated that 28,300 basically trained aircrew would be available to the RAF.

Further recruiting schemes were launched and operated by the various Dominions concerned and the personnel enlisted into the RAAF, RCAF, or RNZAF. Furthermore, large numbers of personnel were recruited in the continent of Africa and trained in schools in South Africa and Southern Rhodesia.

In Southern Rhodesia, personnel from Kenya, Northern and Southern Rhodesia, South Africa, together with Greek and Yugoslav personnel from the Middle East, were enlisted and trained for flying duties within the RAF. In South Africa, the position was somewhat different, as personnel recruited for the South African Air Force did not have any liability to serve outside of the Union, although they were encouraged to volunteer for service with the RAF and SAAF squadrons, and large numbers served with distinction in the Middle Eastern theatres of the war.

Empire Air Training Scheme Agreement

The formal Agreement for the Empire Air Training Scheme (EATS) was signed on the night of 16/17 December 1939. It envisaged twenty-five Elementary Flying Training Schools (EFTSs), twenty-five Service Flying Training Schools (SFTSs), fourteen Air Observers Schools (AOSs), fourteen Bombing & Gunnery Schools (B&GSs), and three Air Navigation Schools (ANSs) to be formed within the three Dominions. The provision of manpower did not of course follow the distribution of schools since some training was to be done in Canada for the other two Dominions.

Canada would supply 51 per cent of the personnel requirements, Australia 37 per cent, and New Zealand 9 per cent, while the UK and Newfoundland the remaining 3 per cent. These personnel requirements were planned to be 11,050 pilots, 6,396 observers, and 10,725 wireless operator/air gunners. The UK undertook to supply almost all the aircraft and engines required, as well as spare parts.

Time was required to build the schools, train the instructors, and provide the aircraft. No time schedules were laid down for Australia or New Zealand, but the Canadian building scheme was to be completed by April 1942. The first output of trained pilots and other aircrew would leave the schools between September and November 1940, and the scheme would reach its maximum capacity by July 1942, and its full output by November 1942. The agreement made with Canada, Australia and New Zealand was to remain in force until 31 March 1943.

Overseas Training Outside the Empire Air Training Scheme

Though the EATS assured the eventual help to the RAF of a substantial number of Dominion Air Force crews, it did nothing to relieve the UK's immediate congestion, nor increase the RAF's own capacity for training. That scheme, however, was not the end of help from the Empire.

Further offers of assistance came from Southern Rhodesia, where it was agreed to form four Elementary and four Service Flying Training Schools, together with a combined school for training both observers and air gunners; and from South Africa where, under the 'Van Brookham' agreement, six Elementary and six Service Flying Training Schools, plus five combined air observer navigation, navigation, bomber, and gunnery schools (known as CAONSs), were to be established.

The pre-war proposal for Kenya was also extended and plans made to set up an Elementary, as well as Service Flying School, in that colony. Other parts of the Empire also responded, and it was proposed to commence small-scale training courses giving elementary flying instruction in Trinidad, Bermuda, the Straits Settlements, Singapore, Hong Kong, and Burma.

By April 1940, the training position was beginning to stabilise. Of the total of around 203 schools required to be in place by 1942 – to supply the estimated front-line squadrons of the RAF – only sixteen were outstanding while more than half of the total schools were located overseas.

Transfer of UK-based RAF Schools Overseas

In May 1940, the German Blitzkrieg in Europe began. The fall of France put an end to any notion of flying training schools in that country, nor Morocco and North Africa for that matter. In the Middle East, the entry into the war of Italy and the start of operations in East Africa caused the EFTS and SFTS planned for Kenya to be transferred to South Africa.

Up to this time, the pattern of basic training organisation had been in two main forms: the Empire Air Training Schemes (EATS) in the Dominions, and the RAF schools. The EATS was developing, and training had begun in all three Dominions. The RAF schools were located mainly in Britain, supplemented by one school in Iran, with some coming into operation in Southern Rhodesia, and some planned for Kenya (which was subsequently moved to South Africa). The South Africa scheme, whereby SAAF training capacity was to be expanded and shared between the SAAF and the RAF, was agreed the following month.

By July 1940, the threat of an imminent attack on the British Isles caused plans to be made of the bodily transfer of RAF schools to overseas locations. In all, seven schools were transferred, four to Canada and three to South Africa.

In South Africa, these three schools were merged with those transferred from Kenya, to form the Joint Air Training Scheme in that Dominion and operated as part of the plan. In Canada, however, the transferred schools remained outside of the EATS and further RAF schools, often referred to as 'Transferred' schools but which were formed by the RAF in Canada, came into effect the following year.

Unfortunately, the various schemes were not due to produce any trained men until the end of 1940, and were then to develop gradually throughout 1941, until 1942 when almost 50,000 aircrew were being trained annually. Unfortunately, the first-line demand for trained men in large numbers was urgent and trained personnel were required before the progress of new schools could turn them out. Consequently, the period of basic training had to be shortened, and then shortened again, in order to turn out the required aircrew within the time. All the schools were working to the RAF syllabus, and so wherever conditions permitted the shortening of courses and the increases in capacities was applied to all schools, regardless of their location. These changes called for more schools and more staff. To compound the problems, training aircraft were in short supply throughout the year and the great distances involved did nothing to improve the supply and administrative problems.

The United States was constantly in mind, not only as a source of aircraft but also as a possible training area with ready-made schools, instructors, and facilities. The question was raised several times during 1940, and while it was not refused, it was turned aside with the remark that 'Canada was a more suitable location'. By the end of the year, however, the refresher schools for training American volunteers for service with the RAF had commenced in the US.

Training in the US

Besides seeing the development of the existing training organisation overseas, 1941 also saw the exploration and development of a new area. Up to this point, all overseas expansion had taken place within the Empire and had followed two main trends: one, where the Dominions trained their own pupils for service in or with the RAF; and the second, the establishment of RAF schools training mainly RAF pupils from the UK for service in the RAF. Both schemes had the same shortcomings: the provision of training aircraft, equipment, and instructional personnel was the responsibility of the RAF. The new source of training facilities in the United States obviated all of these difficulties.

Five different schemes were proposed and developed for training personnel for the RAF and in all cases, the training aircraft, the schools, and the instructional and maintenance personnel were provided by the US. There were still difficulties, of course: pupils were not trained strictly to the RAF syllabus of instruction; administrative problems were not simple; and the American Neutrality Laws caused considerable embarrassment in the early days of American training.

The Refresher Scheme for training US volunteers for service with the RAF was inaugurated in November 1940. The next form of assistance came in March 1941, in the form of a proposal by Pan American Airways to train some RAF observers in their navigation school at Miami. This was closely followed by an offer by the US government to supply training aircraft under Lend-Lease, for use in six civilian flight schools in the US. Known as British Flying Training Schools, these facilities started training RAF pilots in April 1941.

Proposed by General 'Hap' Arnold in April 1941, the 'Arnold Scheme' began training RAF pilots in USAAF schools in June 1941, and shortly afterwards the US Navy offered to train RAF and Fleet Air Arm pilots, as well as observers and wireless operators (air gunners). By the summer of 1941, all five schemes were in operation.

Between June 1941 and March 1943, a total of 7,885 RAF personnel entered the Arnold Scheme, including one Michael Beetham (later Sir Michael Beetham), who became Marshal of the Royal Air Force on 15 October 1982.

US Entry into the War

The Japanese attack on Pearl Harbour on 7 December 1941, and the United States' entry into the war, had an appreciable effect on the overseas training organisation. The immediate effect was the temporary cessation of pupil drafts from Australia and New Zealand to Canada and Southern Rhodesia. It also meant that RAF training in the US could be conducted more openly. After the initial surprise of the attack was overcome, both Australia and New Zealand agreed to maintain their quota of pupils for Canada on the same scale as before, and shipments resumed in March 1942. However, the flow of Australian pupils to Rhodesia was not resumed.

Japanese operations in the Far East put an effective end to the small training operations in Burma and Malaya, and all thoughts for expanding India as a basic training area vanished.

The long-term effects were far more drastic, however. Since the US was in the war, her own forces were anxious to fly American aircraft and this, of course, reduced the numbers allocated to the RAF.

Improved Training Standards

By 1942, the corner had been turned. The requirement to produce trained aircrews at any cost, to meet the demands of the front line, was no longer the overriding factor. At last, sufficient training capacity had been developed, and the shortage of training aircraft and spare parts had been overcome. The peak demand had been reached, but it did not mean that for the remainder of the war years all was plain sailing for the basic training organisations.

The vast, worldwide training organisation that had been built up in the previous two-and-a-half years presented its own special problems. No longer did pilots go straight from their flying training schools to an operational squadron. Transportation considerations, refresher and acclimatisation courses, operational training and conversion, along with other specialist courses, meant there was a considerable time lag between pupils who graduated at overseas training schools reaching the front line.

There was the ever-increasing need for a better standard of training, particularly as the size, power, and complexity of modern aircraft increased and the gap between training and operational aircraft widened. This gap could only be bridged by a higher standard of basic training, especially for both pilots and navigators, and indeed for all crew categories.

That was the pattern of the training organisation until its rundown in 1944. At all schools, syllabuses were improved and modified in the light of operational experience, and course lengths were constantly changing to increase or delay outputs according to the needs of the front line.

Revised EATS Agreement

The Empire Training Scheme of December 1939, which expired in March 1943, was renewed and training continued on a similar basis until 31 March 1945. By the end of 1944, it was the broad policy that most of future basic training would be conducted in the UK, although establishing schools in the UK to replace overseas schools was necessarily a lengthy one, while it was desirable to retain overseas training schools until the UK training capacity had been re-established.

The end of the war with Germany on 8 May 1945 caused a further revision of future training requirements. Since RAF training in Canada and the US was, on account of political and financial considerations, precluded except for war purposes, entry into those schools were planned to cease on 1 July 1945 and those personnel in the system ahead of that date would complete their training programmes.

The End of the War with Japan

When the war with Japan ended on 2 September 1945, further plans for reductions were superimposed on the training programme. All training in Canada and the US was immediately halted, and all pupils under training were returned to the UK. In South Africa and Southern Rhodesia, the authorities were notified that no further pupils would enter training. Anyone undergoing training but not willing to volunteer for an extended programme of RAF service was removed from the training programme.

Effectively, this marked the end of overseas training during the war. Looking to the future, the close cooperation between the air forces of the British Commonwealth that had been apparent during the war continued with some peacetime RAF training in Southern Rhodesia. Meanwhile, discussions continued with Canada, Australia, New Zealand, and South Africa about future joint training arrangements, and interservice co-operation in peacetime.

A navigation instructor, Flight Lieutenant W. A. Blake of Woodstock, Oxfordshire, delivers a lesson on compass deviation to a class of trainees at 33 Air Navigation School, Mount Hope, Ontario, Canada, in September 1942. 33 Air Navigation School was also part of the British Commonwealth Air Training Plan. (*Crown Copyright/Air Historical Branch image CAN-1050*)

Anson I aircraft of 33 Air Navigation School, based at Mount Hope near Hamilton, Ontario, in September 1942. These aircraft were delivered directly from the factory to Canada. Some of the aircraft, including N9559/41, second from left, are still wearing their RAF serial number. (*Crown Copyright/ Air Historical Branch image CAN-1064*)

Former RAF Fairey Battle I aircraft lined up at a snow-covered MacDonald Airfield, Manitoba, Canada, where they were in service with 3 Bombing and Gunnery School. The aircraft second from the left, RCAF serial number 1723, was previously K9355 and is one of a number of Battles fitted with a turret for air gunnery training. (*Crown Copyright/Air Historical Branch image CAN-2307*)

Four Harvard aircraft, including serial numbers 2826, 3232, and 3250, of the RCAF Central Flying School based at Trenton, Ontario. These aircraft were involved in the training of RAF pilots during the British Commonwealth Training Plan. (*Crown Copyright/Air Historical Branch image CAN-2309*)

45

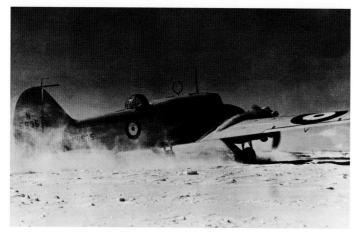

Anson I, N9935, running up its engines in the snow, probably at RCAF Borden, Ontario. This aircraft was given the Canadian serial number 6008 and was later converted as the first Anson III in May 1941, when it was fitted with a pair of 330hp Jacobs L-6MB engines by the National Steel Car Corporation. (*Crown Copyright/Air Historical Branch image CAN-2311*)

Trainee RAF air gunners receiving classroom instruction at an Air Training School in Southern Rhodesia. The instructor is Pilot Officer J. Ward. (*Crown Copyright/Air Historical Branch image CRH-29/ LAC J. H. Adams*)

A training scene from the Rhodesia Air Training Group in August 1943. A Fairey Battle TT.1 provides an airborne target for gunnery students flying behind and below in an Oxford V aircraft. This variant of the Airspeed Oxford was powered by a pair of 450hp Pratt and Witney Wasp Junior engines in place of the original 370hp Armstrong-Siddeley Cheetah X engines. (*Crown Copyright/Air Historical Branch image CRH-33/LAC J. H. Adams*)

Another image from RAF training in Rhodesia during August 1943 shows gunners practicing on a moving target range, towed on the back of a lorry. (*Crown Copyright/Air Historical Branch image CRH-31/LAC J. H. Adams*)

A unidentified Harvard I is prepared for a training flight at a Service Flying Training School, in Southern Rhodesia, in 1943. (*Crown Copyright/Air Historical Branch image CRH-54/LAC J. H. Adams*)

A flying instructor shows a student pilot, Leading Aircraftmen E. W. L. Brice, where he must and must not put his feet when climbing into the cockpit of a Tiger Moth II for his first flying lesson at Bulawayo, Southern Rhodesia. (*Crown Copyright/Air Historical Branch image CRH-115/ LAC J. H. Adams*)

47

North American NA-66 Harvard II, thought to be AJ602/78, taxies from the dispersal during an operational training flight in September 1943. Interestingly, steel helmets were worn during this part of their training. After manufacture in the US, this aircraft was shipped directly to Southern Rhodesia. (*Crown Copyright/Air Historical Branch image CRH-129/LAC J. H. Adams*)

Air Vice Marshal C. W. Meredith, Air Officer Commanding Rhodesia Air Training Group (RATG), takes the salute during a passing out parade at the Initial Training Wing, Bulawayo, Southern Rhodesia, in 1943. (*Crown Copyright/Air Historical Branch image CRH-113/LAC J. H. Adams*)

A PT-17 Stearman flies over Carlstrom Field, Arcadia, Florida, in 1941. The station was home to 5 Basic Flying Training School (5 BFTS) and provided initial flight training to RAF aircrew at the Riddle Aeronautical Institute's facilities. (*Crown Copyright/Air Historical Branch image C-1966*)

A typical scene at Carlstrom Field, Arcadia, Florida, during pilot RAF training in 1941. Lines of PT-17 Stearman aircraft in use with 5 BFTS can be seen. (*Crown Copyright/ Air Historical Branch image C-2167*)

Group Captain D. V. Carnegie, head of the RAF Delegation in Washington DC, congratulates Flight Leader Stonier on being the first RAF cadet to fly from the Riddle Aeronautical Institute's training airfield, at Carlstrom Field, Arcadia, Florida. RAI's Chief Flight Instructor, Jack Hunt, looks on from the front cockpit of the PT-17 Stearman. (*Crown Copyright/Air Historical Branch image C-1957*)

An RAF trainee pilot takes a flying lesson in a Vultee BT-13A, serial number 41-1327, of the US Air Corps Replacement Center, based at Gunter Field, Montgomery, Alabama, in 1941. The center operated as part of the 'Arnold Scheme' from 1941 to 1945. (*Crown Copyright/Air Historical Branch image C-2309*)

Here, an RAF trainee pilot undergoes a briefing ahead of his next instructional flight at Gunter Field, Montgomery, in Vultee BT-13A, serial number 41-1267. (*Crown Copyright/Air Historical Branch image C-2308*)

The A&AEE Joins Training Command (1939–46)

The Curtiss SO3C-2C (named the Seamew in Royal Navy service) was an interesting mid-wing monoplane design capable of operating on either wheels or floats as a shipborne observation aircraft. The Royal Navy ordered 250 Seamew aircraft but the type was noticeably short-lived. Trials of Seamew I, FN475, began in May 1943, when this picture was taken. The Seamew was found to be underpowered, and the trials ended in early 1944. (*Crown Copyright/Air Historical Branch image AAEE-MIS-811-1*)

In 1917, the Experimental Aircraft Flight of the Central Flying School was transferred from Upavon to a site on the heathland at Martlesham Heath. Shortly afterwards, on 16 January 1917, Martlesham Heath airfield was officially opened as an experimental airfield. The unit was later renamed the Aeroplane Experimental Unit, Royal Flying Corps, and continued to operate at Martlesham Heath.

On 16 March 1920, it was renamed the Aeroplane Experimental Establishment (Home) as part of No. 3 Group, RAF. It continued to operate from Martlesham Heath with a detachment at nearby Orfordness. During the next four years it was moved into No. 1 Group (31 August 1921), into Coastal Area (1 February 1922), and into Inland Area on 1 April 1923, before being redesignated the Aeroplane & Armament Experimental Establishment on 24 March 1924 for trials and evaluation of aircraft and armament.

On 14 January 1926, the organisation was divided into two separate squadrons: 15 Squadron (Armament and Testing) and 22 Squadron (performance and Handling). However, on 1 May 1934, it was further reorganised as the Armament Testing Squadron and Performance Testing Squadron with 22 Squadron being disbanded in the process. Just one month later, on 1 June 1932, 15 Squadron was also removed.

Wartime Changes

Considerable concern had been raised regarding the proximity of Martlesham Heath's location on the East Coast and its vulnerability to enemy attack. At the outbreak of the Second World War, on 9 September 1939, the A&AEE was moved to a site at Boscombe Down, Wiltshire, as part of 23 Group, in turn part of RAF Training Command. Around fifty aircraft, along with both civilian and military personnel, arrived at Boscombe Down by the middle of September 1939 and it was officially declared 'open' on 20 September by the new Commanding Officer, Group Captain B. McEntegart.

Initially, the A&AEE shared the facility with 'D' Flight, the Radio Direction Finding experimental organisation, but this was soon moved north to Perth, where it was redesignated Station Flight. Primarily for security reasons, this was soon changed to 'A' Flight of the Special Duty Flight.

In September 1939, resources at the airfield were limited at best, being just a grass field, a small area of hardstanding, five pre-1930s hangars along with a single new one, and some other permanent structures. Sadly, what it clearly lacked was any access to ranges necessary for the testing of weapons. It also lacked sufficient domestic and working accommodation, so the new residents initially struggled to make themselves at home, especially when occupying the temporary wooden huts tucked away on the south side of the airfield.

The main group of fifty-one A&AEE aircraft arrived at Boscombe Down on 3 September, while a second group of nineteen arrived on the following day, although it is not clear exactly how many aircraft were initially based there. The Operations Record Book states that it was fifty-two. It could have been even lower if the Army had been a little more accurate when they opened first on the first aircraft to approach their new base.

New Hard Runway for Boscombe Down – Eventually!

When the A&AEE moved into the airfield in September 1939, it was just a field, much of it on a downhill slope with some rough and uneven patches. Take-offs and landings could be made in any direction, the longest 'runway' measuring around 1,800 yards orientated NW/SE, which was particularly vulnerable to a south-easterly wind, which could mean landing down the slope. Continuous operations of the airfield did not see any improvements; in fact, over time it became rutted and uneven, leading to the loss and damage to several aircraft, including the prototype Halifax, Mosquito, Liberator and Typhoon.

Sadly, these incidents were to continue until a new, hard surface could be completed, although this was not commissioned until early 1945 and even then access onto and off the runway remained hazardous. Verbal representations to the Air Ministry had been followed up with a formal approach in February 1943 before work commenced the following January. Initially, it was to be 7,500 feet in length, orientated as 24/06, although this was later extended post-war to 10,529 feet, while a second runway of 6,280 feet was later added to the facility.

New Ranges

Another problem with the move to Boscombe Down was the almost complete lack of weapons ranges in the vicinity. Bombing ranges were available with the Chemical Defence Experimental Station at Porton and the Army at Larkhill. Neither was under the direct control of the A&AEE and when access was required it needed to be booked in advance; even then, both was often unavailable.

The A&AEE had their own bombing range at Crichel Down before the end of 1939. Located almost 5 miles north-east of Blandford and around 1,800 yards in diameter, it eventually had two bombing targets; the first for low-level targets while the second suited testing of high-level targets, although bombs were limited to 1,000-pounds in weight, while heights of up to 14,000 feet for inert weapons were permitted.

There was a live firing and bombing facility in the sea at Lyme Bay, off the south coast, that later tested the firing of rocket projectiles. The area was around 12 miles in length, extending to 6 miles out to sea and there were no limitations on operations once the area had been confirmed free of ships.

The next range was at Ashley Walk, near Fordingbridge in the New Forest. Controlled by the A&AEE, it occupied an area of 3½ miles by 1½ miles and eventually housed up to ten targets. Here, the maximum dropping height was 20,000 feet, although all incendiary devices were excluded due to the high risk of fires among the heather. That said, the range did test the live firing of a 22,000-pound 'Grand Slam' bomb, which left a particularly large crater.

Recognition Photographs

During wartime an additional task provided by the A&AEE was obtaining air-to-air photographs of new aircraft as they arrived for testing. These images were of particular use in providing recognition details of 'friendly' aircraft to the fighter pilots and gun operators.

The necessity for the photographs became clearly apparent when, in May 1940, a 'new' and unarmed Stirling bomber operating with the A&AEE from Boscombe Down was twice attacked over the English Channel by Spitfire aircraft, despite the crew firing every recognition Very cartridge on board until the attackers finally relented.

Perhaps, more interestingly, this wealth of historic and high-quality photographic images has provided numerous authors and publishers with a spectacular selection of images of all kinds of aircraft under test with the A&AEE, as well as a variety of captured Luftwaffe types, and a good number of these are reproduced in the following pages.

Variety of Aircraft Tested at the A&AEE

Due to the specific nature of the work conducted at Boscombe Down by the A&AEE, the organisation was particularly busy throughout the war. Aside from the 'Armament' aspect of their title, the 'Aeroplane' part meant examining performance, handling, engineering, flame damping, contamination, radio, navigation and, initially, photographic assessment. All aircraft were flown by the Performance Testing Squadron, with its three flights.

Of particular interest was the operational testing of bombers, including the new four-engine aircraft as these soon revealed capabilities well below those originally expected by Bomber Command – the Halifax being a particular case in question, as was to a lesser extent, the Stirling Mk 1, although work by the A&AEE did improve its performance.

On the 'Armament' side of things, the Bombing Flight had fourteen aircraft on strength in 1939, including five Blenheim aircraft, with which to conduct trials on a variety of ordnance. During later years, the Lancaster became the vehicle of choice, particularly as it was the only aircraft capable of carrying and releasing the larger weapons. During the war, the ordnance increased considerably in size with the testing of the 'Capital Ship' bomb of 5,000 pounds in 1942 and the 22,000-pound 'Grand Slam' weapon, of which only a single live drop was conducted at Ashley Walk, in front of designer Dr Barnes Wallis.

Aside from captured Luftwaffe designs, the variety of aircraft tested by the A&AEE during the war included heavy, medium, and light bombers; maritime, transport and training aircraft; single and multi-seat fighters; as well as a range of aircraft destined for service with the Royal Navy – many of which never entered service due to serious shortcomings in one form or another.

A limited selection of aircraft tested at the A&AEE can be seen in the following images on pages 54 to 60.

Transfer to the Ministry of Supply

In 1946, the A&AEE left the command of RAF Flying Training Command, and in common with other military research establishments, came directly under the Ministry of Supply.

Gloster F.5/34 prototype, K5604, photographed in June 1937 but did not make its maiden flight until December. It was one of two prototypes that flew very successfully, but the design lost out to the Hurricane and Spitfire – which had been pre-ordered before the competition! After the trials had concluded, the maintenance serial 1749M was allocated in December 1939 and the aircraft continued in use as an instructional airframe with No. 3 School of Technical Training. (*Crown Copyright/Air Historical Branch image ATP-9130c*)

Curtiss Cleveland I, AS467, photographed in August 1940. The aircraft, designed as a dive bomber and named the 'Helldiver' in US Navy service, was originally part of a contract destined for the French Navy. Sadly, when France fell in June 1940, the aircraft were diverted to Martinique where they sat out the war. Five aircraft from that contract were diverted to the UK and allocated the serial numbers AS467–471, and were briefly tested at the A&AEE during this time. (*Crown Copyright/Air Historical Branch image AAEE-9651*)

The Stinson L-1 Vigilant was a light observation aircraft built by the Stinson Aircraft Company. By 1940, Stinson had become a division of Vultee Aircraft. The design was operated by the US Army as the O-49 until 1942. HL430 was one of four Vultee Vigilant I aircraft (HL429–432) delivered in late 1941. Up to seventeen L-1 and ninety-six L-1A airframes had been allocated to the RAF under the Lend-Lease Act. HL430 remained with the A&AEE but the remaining order and proposed large batch was cancelled. (*Crown Copyright/Air Historical Branch image AAEE-MIS-VIGILANT-2*)

When Luftwaffe Junkers Ju88A-5 M2+MK (c/n 6073) landed in error at Chivenor on 26 November 1941, it was duly captured. It was allocated the RAF serial HM509 and later sent to Boscombe Down where it underwent engine flame damping trials during the following year. (*Crown Copyright/Air Historical Branch image AAEE-MIS-710-1*)

Folland F.43/37 P1775 was one of twelve F.43 aircraft (P1774 to P1786) ordered by the RAF specifically as engine test beds and was photographed at Boscombe Down in March 1942. It is seen here with a Bristol Hercules VIII engine installed but was later flown with the Centaurus IV. (*Crown Copyright/ Air Historical Branch image AAEE-MIS-F4337*)

Former Luftwaffe Focke-Wulf FW.190A-4/U-8 (c/n 7155) was captured when its pilot landed in error at West Malling on 17 April 1943. The aircraft was allocated the RAF serial PE882 and was photographed on 26 June 1943 in the hands of Brian Purvis, a test pilot from at the A&AEE at Boscombe Down. (*Crown Copyright/Air Historical Branch image AAEE-AC-171d*)

The sole Boulton Paul P92/2, V3142, pictured during handling tests with the A&AEE on 3 July 1943. The P92/2 was a half-scale aerodynamic testbed built to specification F11/37 by the Heston Aircraft Company for a proposed twin-engine fighter that was cancelled in August 1940, although V3142 continued to serve in flight test duties with the A&AEE. (*Crown Copyright/Air Historical Branch image AAEE-PS-1-112*)

Grumman F6F-3 Gannet FN323 pictured during performance and handling trials with the A&AEE in June 1943. All Royal Navy Gannet aircraft were later renamed 'Hellcat' in January 1944. (*Crown Copyright/Air Historical Branch image AAEE-PS-1-57*)

The Westland P.14 Welkin was designed to fight at very high altitudes to counter the threat of the Junkers Ju 86 bombers flying high-altitude reconnaissance missions over the UK, which led to the perception that the Luftwaffe may attempt to bomb the UK from very high altitude. DX282, a production standard Welkin, was photographed while undergoing trials at Boscombe Down in November 1943. Ten of these high-altitude aircraft were flown at various times at Boscombe Down and five crashed, with four aircraft being written off as a result. One of those written off was DX282, which arrived in November 1943 and was force-landed a few days following problems with the port engine over speeding. A further accident was suffered just two weeks later. The aircraft was eventually written off following a crash on take-off in January 1944 when the port engine failed. (*Crown Copyright/Air Historical Branch image AAEE-MIS-808-3*)

The Northrop P-61A Black Widow was the first operational US warplane designed as a night fighter, and the first aircraft designed to use radar. 42-5486 was loaned from the US Army Air Force in May 1944 for trials at Boscombe Down, which lasted a total of thirty hours. (*Crown Copyright/Air Historical Branch image ATP-11782b*)

DX255 was one of four Bristol Buckingham prototypes (DX248, 255, 259 and 266) and was photographed in July 1944. Tested as a light bomber, the Buckingham showed some promise, but the trials revealed stability problems, which led to the enlargement of the twin fins. The Centaurus engines also proved problematic when running hot. The project was cancelled in August 1944. (*Crown Copyright/Air Historical Branch image AAEE-MIS-816-1*)

One of the early Douglas A-26B Invaders (serial number 41-39158) that had been delivered to Britain for service with the USAAF was tested by the A&AEE at Boscombe Down beginning in July 1944. Following these tests, the RAF was allocated an initial batch of 140 A-26Cs. They were designated Invader I and were assigned RAF serials KL690/KL829. They were delivered to the Mediterranean theatre with 2 Group and replaced the Boston aircraft being operated by 88 Squadron, as well as those of 342 Squadron of the Free French Air Force. (*Crown Copyright/Air Historical Branch image AAEE-MIS-823-1*)

The prototype Avro Lincoln I, PW925, photographed while undergoing handling trials with the A&AEE in July 1944. The aircraft was later allocated the maintenance serial 6141M and ended its days as an instructional airframe. (*Crown Copyright/Air Historical Branch image AAEE-PS-1-156*)

Gloster G.41 Meteor I, serial number EE212/G, was photographed while undergoing handling trials with the A&AEE on 26 September 1944. Interestingly, the '/G' presentation of the serial denoted that the aircraft was always to have an armed guard while it was on the ground. (*Crown Copyright/Air Historical Branch image AAEE-PS-1-59*)

Built by the English Electric Company to an order placed in May 1944, TG274/G was the first production de Havilland DH.100 Vampire I, of an initial batch of 120 aircraft. It was photographed at Boscombe Down in February 1945. (*Crown Copyright/Air Historical Branch image AAEE-MIS-819-1*)

Post-war Flying Training Command (1946–55)

The de Havilland Vampire T.11 marked the beginning of a new era in Flying Training Command when it became the first jet aircraft on which RAF pilots actually qualified for their 'wings'. It entered service in 1952 with Advanced Flying Training Schools at RAF Valley and Weston Zoyland before joining No. 5 FTS at RAF Oakington in May 1954. This example, WZ507, is the only remaining airworthy Vampire T.11 and flies with Vampire Preservation in the UK as G-VTII. (*Keith Wilson/SFB Photographic image 2-0115*)

At the end of the Second World War, the immediate task for the RAF was to return to normal, peacetime conditions. For the second time in its history, the RAF was faced with the problems of adjusting to peace after a major war. At the conclusion of the war, the total strength of UK service personnel totalled almost 5 million, with the RAF contingent estimated at around 1.3 million. Various statistics are available, each providing variations, but one RAF source document suggests that the total number of aircraft held on strength (including those in storage) amounted to 61,584.

The rundown of the RAF was more orderly and gradual than it had been in 1919 and by 1947. Almost a million men and women had been demobilised and the overall strength was below 300,000 while aircraft held on strength had reduced drastically to 20,430.

Unsurprisingly, this period saw a significant reduction in the size of RAF Flying Training Command. The post-war RAF was quite different from the organisation that had entered the war in 1939. A revised peacetime structure was required which reflected a new organisation going forward, especially with the advent of jet aircraft. Many, if not all the specialist wartime training units would have little purpose in what was to become a drastically reduced organisation.

Another major problem was the retention of key personnel. The post-war demobilisation process had seen vast numbers removed, while many were remaining only as part of the RAF Volunteer Reserve, although many were waiting for demobilisation and their opportunity to return to civilian life. Some were willing to remain with the RAF, but they were not necessarily the ones the RAF would prefer to retain. Some that did remain had to serve at a lower rank and lose the benefits of their temporarily acquired wartime ranks.

Immediate Rundown

When the war with Japan ended on 2 September 1945, all training undertaken by the overseas training programmes in both Canada and the US was immediately halted, with all pupils being returned to the UK. In South Africa and Southern Rhodesia, those pupils already undergoing training but not willing to volunteer for an extended programme of service were removed from training; while the remainder could complete their courses, effectively marking the end of overseas training.

CFS Resurrected but EFTS Decimated

On a more positive note, the Central Flying School had been resurrected at Little Rissington in May 1946 by combining 7 Flying Instructors School (Advanced) from Upavon with 10 Flying Instructors School (Elementary) from Woodley. The merger was ideal in theory but in practice the facilities at Little Rissington were too small for both levels. Consequently, the school divided with the CFS (Advanced Section) remaining at Little Rissington, while the CFS (Elementary Section) moved across to South Cerney.

The Pilot Training organisation was decimated with many Elementary Flying Training Schools (EFTSs) being closed, while those that remained did so in an almost skeletal form until a new, peacetime reserve organisation could once again be created. However, when the structure was put into place, they were renamed Reserve Flying Schools (RFS). For example, No. 1 EFTS became No. 1 Reserve Flying School on 5 May 1947.

With this reorganisation of the EFTSs, the process of training service pupil pilots now reverted to the Service Flying Training Schools (SFTS). The new SFTSs became all-through Flying Training Schools and, in a similar manner to the EFTSs, they often retained their existing number. For example, No. 3 Service Flying Training School at RAF Feltwell became No. 3 FTS on 9 April 1947. At the time it was equipped primarily with Harvard IIB aircraft, as well as a few Tiger Moth T.2 aircraft, although the latter gave way to the new Prentice T.1 by the end of 1948.

The RAF College at Cranwell had remained in existence throughout the war, but in April 1947 it absorbed the then resident 19 FTS to reform its flying training element, which had been lost in the latter days of the war. In June 1949, an RAF Flying College was formed at RAF Manby, which soon absorbed the Empire Air Armament School located there. It also absorbed functions of the Empire Flying School at Hullavington, aside from the Examining Wing, which had been transferred to the CFS.

Despite the significant reduction in size, the Command did benefit from several new training aircraft types it received into service during the ten years following the end of the Second World War. Many of these designs incorporated lessons learned from war time training, while others represented the next generation of aircraft for the RAF, including the first jet training aircraft.

Prentice Replaces Tiger Moth and Magister

Designed to Air Ministry Specification T.23/43, the prototype Prentice (TV163) made its first flight on 31 March 1946. The design incorporated new ideas gleaned from the wartime training experience of pilot-training techniques and was significantly different from the low-powered lementary trainers – Tiger Moth and Magister – then in service, as it had a more powerful ?51hp engine along with a variable-pitch propeller, flaps, and radio. It provided a side-by-side raining set up and was the RAF's first basic training aircraft configured with that layout.

Almost 400 Prentice T.1 aircraft were ordered for the RAF and entered service with the Basic Training Squadrons of the Central Flying School at South Cerney, at the RAF College at Cranwell, as well as Flying Training Squadrons at Ternhill, Cottesmore, Feltwell and elsewhere. The type was also used for the training of air signallers at RAF Swanton Morley for several years.

Athena and Balliol

The Boulton Paul Balliol was initially designed to meet Air Ministry Specification T.7/45, which called for a three-seat advanced training aircraft powered by a single turboprop engine. The first prototype, VL892, was temporarily fitted with an 820hp Bristol Mercury 30 engine and made its first flight on 30 May 1947. The second aircraft, VL917, made its first flight on 24 March 1948 and become the first aircraft to fly powered solely by single turboprop engine – in this case an Armstrong Siddeley Mamba.

Trials continued and a decision was taken to revert to a more conventional two-seat conventional piston-powered training aircraft. The powerplant chosen was a Rolls-Royce Merlin 35 and four prototypes were constructed using this engine, with the first, VW897, flying on 10 July 1948. This version was designated Balliol T.2 and a batch of seventeen aircraft were ordered to replace the remaining Harvard aircraft in RAF service. Large contracts were placed for the Balliol T.2 but these were cut back in 1951, when further changes in air-training policy favoured the introduction of a jet for advanced training. As a result, production of the Balliol T.2 totalled just 162, with only one Flying Training School – 7 FTS at Cottesmore – operating the type. It later served with the RAF College at Cranwell until superseded by the Vampire in 1956. The last Balliol T.2 aircraft served the RAF with 288 Squadron and 238 OCU.

While the Balliol was being developed, a competitive design – the Avro Athena T.2 – was also being developed to specification T.7/45. The first prototype T.2, VW890, developed from the earlier Mamba-powered T.1, made its first flight on 1 August 1948. Just eleven Athena T.2 aircraft were supplied to the RAF and were used mainly by the Flying College at Manby between 1950 and 1955.

First Jet Trainer Enters RAF Service

In December 1948, the Meteor T.7 became the first jet trainer to enter Flying Training Command service. Its introduction coincided with the virtual completion of Fighter Command's re-equipping with the Meteor F.4 and FB.5 as squadron standard equipment. The only piston-powered aircraft remaining in squadron service being the night-flying Mosquito along with a few Spitfire aircraft with the RAuxAF.

The trainer variant had been developed by Gloster as a private venture, with the prototype (G-AKPK) making its first flight on 19 March 1948. The first Meteor T.7 for RAF service (VW410) made its first flight on 26 October 1948, and more than 640 were built before construction ceased with XF279 in July 1954.

Within Flying Training Command, the Meteor T.7 was employed at a number of Advanced Flying Schools and utilised for the conversion of pilots who had completed their basic flying training on either Harvard or Balliol aircraft. The first course was run by 203 AFS at RAF Driffield in August 1949. Similar courses were run by Advanced Flying Schools at Middle St George, Oakington, Full Sutton, Merryfield, Weston Zoyland, Tarrant Rushton, Worksop,

Finningley, as well as Operational Conversion Units at Stradishall, Leeming, Chivenor, and Bassingbourn. The Meteor T.7 remained in service up until 1956/57, and towards the end of its life usually operated alongside the Vampire T.11.

Valetta T.3

The Valetta was designed to Air Ministry Specification C.9/46 as a military variant of the Viking civil airliner, a small number of which had served with the King's Flight in 1947. The prototype Valetta (VL262) made its first flight on 30 June 1947 with the first production C.1 variant flying on 28 January 1948. A C.2 variant was also developed as a VIP transport aircraft.

Vickers later developed the T.3 variant – effectively a 'flying classroom' to Specification T.1/49 for the training of navigators. This variant made its first flight on 31 August 1950 and forty entered service with five Air Navigation Schools, as well as the RAF College at Cranwell. Sixteen of the T.3 variants were later modified to T.4 specification by Marshall's of Cambridge, equipped with a long radar nose. Most of these served with 228 OCU at RAF Leeming. By the time production of the Valetta ceased, the RAF had taken a total of 262 into service.

Varsity In and Wellington Out

The Varsity T.1 was designed as a replacement for the Wellington T.10 crew training aircraft, to Air Ministry Specification T.13/48. Similar to the earlier Viking and Valetta, the new design featured a tricycle undercarriage, bringing it in line with more modern, conventional aircraft. The prototype Varsity made its first flight on 17 July 1949 and a production order was soon placed. First deliveries to the RAF were made in October 1951, when the Varsity T.1 replaced the Wellington at 201 Advanced Flying School at RAF Swinderby.

The Varsity was employed by Flying Training Command as both a conversion trainer for pilots proceeding onto heavier, multi-piston-engine types, and as a platform for the advanced instruction of navigators and bomb aimers. Production of the Varsity T.1 ended on 24 February 1954 after a total of 160 aircraft had been delivered. The Varsity T.1 continued to serve the RAF into the 1970s, when most aircraft were concentrated with 6 FTS at RAF Finningley, until they began being replaced by the Jetstream in 1974. The Varsity T.1 was finally withdrawn from Flying Training Schools in 1976.

The RAF's last Wellington T.10, MF428, was retired in October 1952 and flown to RAF St Athan for storage. The aircraft is now preserved at the RAF Museum Hendon.

Chipmunk becomes *ab initio* Trainer

The Chipmunk was designed by de Havilland of Canada at Toronto and made its first flight on 22 May 1946. A total of 158 were manufactured in Canada, mainly for the RCAF.

Following test flying at Boscombe Down with two Canadian-built examples – G-AJVD and G-AKDN – the Air Ministry decided to adopt the type as its *ab intio* training aircraft to Specification 8/48. Production of the RAF aircraft, now designated Chipmunk T.10, began (at Hatfield) with WB549. In total, the RAF ordered 735 aircraft, with production at both Hatfield and later at Broughton, near Chester. The last aircraft – WZ884 – was delivered on 1 October 1953.

The first Chipmunk T.10 aircraft were delivered to the Oxford University Air Squadron in February 1950, where they succeeded the Tiger Moth at Kidlington. Thereafter, the Chipmunk became standard equipment with all seventeen University Air Squadrons, while it was also chosen to serve as the basic training aircraft with all twenty Reserve Flying Schools, until these were closed in 1953 as an economy measure.

The venerable Chipmunk remained in RAF service, providing valuable service as a basic trainer, until the final aircraft were withdrawn in the mid-1990s. Two Chipmunk T.10 aircraft remain with the Battle of Britain Memorial Flight at RAF Coningsby, where they provide valuable tailwheel continuity training to the pilots on the flight.

Vampire Introduces a New Era

The arrival of the de Havilland Vampire T.11 in 1952 marked the beginning of a new era for Flying Training Command when it became the first jet aircraft on which RAF pilots actually qualified for their 'wings'. Before the arrival of the Vampire T.11, this stage of training was the domain of the piston-powered Harvard.

Under the previous system, pilots left the Flying Training School with no jet experience, which was deferred until the Advanced Flying School stage on Meteor T.7 aircraft. With the introduction of the Provost/Vampire sequence in 1953, the Advanced Flying Schools were gradually closed as jet-trained pilots left their FTS ready for an Operational Conversion Unit (OCU).

The prototype Vampire Trainer (WW456) was produced at the Airspeed works at Christchurch (then a de Havilland subsidiary) and made its first flight on 15 November 1950. The first production T.11 (WW458) flew on 1 December 1951, and was later delivered to the Royal Navy. The first aircraft for the RAF was WZ414. Total RAF orders for the T.11 reached 530 aircraft, with the last being XK637.

The aircraft initially entered service with Advanced Flying Schools at Valley and Weston Zoyland in 1952, while later deliveries went to 5 FTS at Oakington where the first Provost/Vampire course began in May 1954. Later, in 1956, the Vampire T.11 replaced the Balliol aircraft at the RAF College Cranwell.

The Vampire T.11 made its last operational sortie in RAF service on 29 November 1967, when a flight of four provided a farewell aerobatic display at RAF Leeming.

Piston Provost

The Provost T.1 was designed to Air Ministry Specification T.16/48 and was selected as the standard basic trainer of the RAF in 1953, where it replaced the Prentice in Flying Training Command. The type made its first flight on 24 November 1950, powered by a 385hp Armstrong Siddeley Cheetah 18 engine, although this powerplant was later replaced with the 550hp Alvis Leonides 126 engine in production aircraft.

After a competition with the Handley Page HPR.2, an initial production order for 200 aircraft was placed in February 1951, although this was later increased to a total of 397 aircraft.

With the arrival into service of the Provost T.1, the RAF was able to introduce an entirely new training scheme for pilot training based around the combination of Provost T.1 and Vampire T.11; thereby replacing the Prentice/Harvard system that had been in use since 1948.

First deliveries were to the Central Flying School's Basic Training Squadron at South Cerney, while the first Flying Training School to be fully equipped with the Provost was at Ternhill, where the first course commenced in October 1953.

With the emergence of the Jet Provost T.1, the Provost was gradually withdrawn from flying schools, although a few did soldier on with the Central Air Traffic Control School at RAF Shawbury and the last – WW397 – was retired in November 1969.

Jet Provost T.1

With the establishment of the Provost T.1/Vampire T.11 training programme in Flying Training Command, requiring the transition from a piston-powered basic trainer to a jet advanced trainer, the next logical step was to move to a jet basic trainer – thereby permitting an advent of 'all-through jet training'. Hunting Percival saw this opportunity and offered the Air Ministry a private venture design for consideration.

In March 1953, the Ministry of Supply placed an order on behalf of the RAF, for nine of these aircraft, known as the Jet Provost T.1, for testing. The first prototype (XD674) made its first flight on 16 June 1954, and shortly afterwards the order was increased to ten Jet Provost T.1 aircraft, all of which were delivered to examine its capabilities to undertake primary jet training. From August 1955, these trials were held at 2 FTS at RAF Hullavington, with a particular view to examining the possible concept of an all-through jet training syllabus. The first pupil to go solo on a Jet Provost T.1 was Pilot Officer R. T. Foster on 17 October 1955.

While the Jet Provost T.1 design did not set the RAF's training world alight, it did prove the all-through jet training concept and began a long association with the Jet Provost in its later T.3, T.4 and T.5 forms.

On the Horizon

While the period from 1946 to 1955 had seen a significant reduction in pilot training, it had pioneered significant changes in training equipment while also introducing the very first all-through jet training. These influences were to have a major impact on pilot training during the following years.

In 1946, a new system of coding for aircraft in Flying Training, Technical Training and Reserve Commands was introduced, which comprised a four-letter code. The first letter (F, R or T) stood for the Command, the second and third letter denoted the unit, while the fourth identified the individual aircraft. Number 3 Flying Training School at RAF Feltwell were allocated six different unit codes (FBP, Q, R, S, T and U) to accommodate all the aircraft operated by them including Prentice T.1, Tiger Moth T.2, Anson T.1, Magister T.1 and Harvard T.2B. The four Harvard T.2B aircraft in this image shot on 10 April 1948 are FX294/FBU-S, KF162/FBS-D, KF430/FBT-K and KF966/FBR-M. (*Crown Copyright/Air Historical Branch image R-1400*)

Bristol Buckmaster T.1, RP246/FCV-E, of the Empire Flying School based at RAF Hullavington, was photographed in 1947. This aircraft had a short service life and only served with this unit (including its predecessor, the Empire Central Flying School) between April 1946 and October 1949 before being withdrawn from service and used for instructional duties at RAF St Athan. (*Crown Copyright/Air Historical Branch image PRB-1-727*)

De Havilland Mosquito FB.VI, TA588/FJT-Y, of the Central Gunnery School based at RAF Leconfield, firing a salvo of rocket projectiles during a training sortie on 18 November 1948. Codes allocated to the school post-war were in the range 'FJR' to 'FJX'. (*Crown Copyright/Air Historical Branch image R-1970*)

The Central Gunnery School at RAF Leconfield had an interesting assortment of aircraft on their strength in the post-war period including this Spitfire LF.XVI RW396/FJW-L, also photographed on 18 November 1948. (*Crown Copyright/ Air Historical Branch image R-1979*)

Air-to-ground gunnery practice against a floating target using Lancaster B.VII NX776/FGA-D from the Air Armament School at RAF Manby on 18 November 1948. (*Crown Copyright/ Air Historical Branch image R-1976*)

Avro Lincoln B.2, RF523, named *Thor II*, of the Empire Air Armament School based at RAF Manby, pictured over the East Coast of England in mid-1949. This unit was absorbed into the RAF College on 31 July 1949. (*Crown Copyright/ Air Historical Branch image R-2409*)

The Boulton Paul Balliol T.2 was built to specification T.14/47. Originally designed with an Armstrong Siddeley Mamba turboprop engine, it was later re-engined with a Rolls-Royce Merlin 35 (as seen here). The first prototype (VW897) made its first flight on 10 July 1948. The type only served in the training role with 7FTS at Cottesmore and the RAF College Cranwell for a short period of time (1952–55), owing to the emergence of jet training aircraft. VW899 was the third prototype and was photographed in 1950. (*Crown Copyright/Air Historical Branch image PRB-1-814*)

The prototype Vickers Varsity T.1 aircrew trainer, VX828, built to specification T.13/48, made its first flight on 17 July 1949. Developed from the earlier Vickers Valetta, the Varsity served with a number of flying training and air navigation schools until mid-1976 when replaced by the Handley Page Jetstream T.1. This image was taken in 1950. (*Crown Copyright/Air Historical Branch image PRB-1-816*)

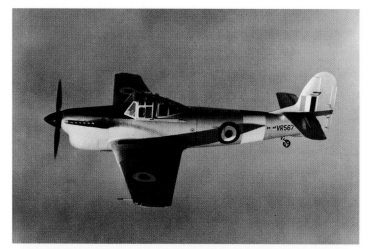

Avro Athena T.2, VR567, of the Central Gunnery School at RAF Manby was photographed on 22 September 1950. The Athena was the losing design in a competition for a two-seat advanced trainer held in 1948/9, which was won by the Balliol T.2. Only eleven Athena T.2 aircraft served at RAF Manby between 1950 and 1955. (*Crown Copyright/Air Historical Branch image PRB-1-859*)

In December 1948, the Meteor T.7 became the first jet trainer to go into service with the RAF. The first conversion course within Flying Training Command began with 203 AFS at RAF Driffield and commenced in August 1949. This image shows four Meteor T.7 aircraft from that unit in June 1951. (*Crown Copyright/ Air Historical Branch image PRB-1-2508*)

This image shows a line of Anson T.21 aircraft (including VV330, VV950 and VV963) of No. 1 Basic Air Navigation School as they run up their engines at the start of another day's flying at Hamble on 16 August 1951. (*Crown Copyright/Air Historical Branch image PRB-1-3108*)

The Percival Prentice T.1 superseded the veteran Tiger Moth in Flying Training Command in 1948 and remained in service until the arrival of the Provost T.1 in 1953. This image shows four Prentice T.1 aircraft of 3FTS (including VS246/FBP-X, VS279/FBR-M and VS349/FBP-D) at RAF Feltwell in July 1951. (*Crown Copyright/Air Historical Branch image PRB-1-3007*)

The second prototype Percival P.56 Provost, WE530, photographed during late 1952. The Provost was the RAF's last piston-engine basic trainer aircraft ordered by the RAF and its introduction with Flying Training Schools from 1953 onwards allowed the RAF to introduce a new flying training syllabus with pilots receiving instruction on the Provost T.1 before proceeding to the Vampire jet-powered advanced trainer. (*Crown Copyright/Air Historical Branch image PRB-1-5789*)

The Meteor T.7 Aerobatic Team of 203 Advanced Flying School, RAF Driffield, which performed before HRH the Duke of Edinburgh at the RAF College Cranwell on 28 July 1953. The team, consisting of Meteor T.7 aircraft WL413/X-68, WF881/X-55, WF776/X-54 and WL361/X-71, were photographed in flight shortly before being disbanded in October of that year. (*Crown Copyright/Air Historical Branch image PRB-1-7011*)

Handley Page Marathon T.11, XA274, photographed in flight on 24 September 1953. In 1951, the Air Ministry ordered twenty-eight Marathon aircraft for the RAF (XA249–XA276) and the first aircraft made its maiden flight on 29 August 1952. The Marathon T.11 had a relatively short career, and all had been withdrawn from RAF service by June 1958. (*Crown Copyright/Air Historical Branch image PRB-1-6922*)

Following the end of the Second World War, 270 Wellington X aircraft were reconditioned by Boulton Paul for service as crew trainers with Flying Training Command, particularly with the Air Navigation Schools. The type was later superseded by the Valetta T.3 and all Wellington T.10 aircraft were withdrawn from RAF service by 1953. The RAF's last Wellington T.10, MF428, had been delivered to No. 1 Air Navigation School at RAF Hullavington in April 1949, where it remained until retired in October 1952 and flown to RAF St Athan for storage. The aircraft is now preserved at the RAF Museum Hendon. The RAF's last Wellington was pictured during its very last service flight in October 1953. (*Crown Copyright/Air Historical Branch image PRB-1-7028*)

Vickers Valetta T.3 navigational training aircraft, WG259/A, was photographed in flight on 22 March 1954. The Valetta T.3 was a 'flying classroom' version of the Valetta C.1 transport design and was used to train navigators, hence the line of six astrodomes fitted to the upper fuselage. The Valetta T.3 served with five air navigation schools as well as the RAF College at Cranwell. WG259/A served with 2 ANS at RAF Thorney Island. (*Crown Copyright/Air Historical Branch image PRB-1-7578*)

A Provost T.1, WV429/N-Z, flies alongside a Vampire T.11, XD520, on 9 June 1954. The Provost was from 6FTS at RAF Ternhill while the Vampire came from 206 AFS at RAF Oakington. The combination of Provost T.1 and Vampire T.11 represented the RAF's new flying training syllabus. (*Crown Copyright/Air Historical Branch image T-10*)

The Jet Provost T.1 prototype, XD674, flies in formation with the camership as it makes it way to the 1954 Farnborough air show, held at the Hampshire airfield from 6 to 12 September. The wide side-by-side cockpit of the new jet training platform is clearly visible in this view. (*Crown Copyright/ Air Historical Branch image PRB-1-8676a*)

In July 1954, Nos 3 and 4 Civilian Anti-aircraft Co-operation Units were amalgamated to become 3/4 CAACU at Exeter, when it formed part of 25 Group, Flying Training Command. This image shows Mosquito TT.35, TA719/56, photographed at its base at Exeter. Originally built in 1945 as a Mosquito B.35, it was converted to Target Towing configuration by Brooklands Aviation in 1953. When the aircraft was finally withdrawn from service in 1963, it participated in the making of the film *633 Squadron* before being placed into storage with No. 27 MU at Shawbury. It was later donated to the Imperial War Museum at Duxford, where it is preserved today. (*Rod Brown*)

A variety of Auster and Taylorcraft variants including the Mk 1, AOP.V, AOP.6, T.7 and AOP.9 have seen service within Flying Training and Training Command over the years, although most seem to have avoided the camera. TW455 was photographed at White Waltham on 30 May 1955. The aircraft was struck off charge on 16 December 1955 and registered G-AOJL, before being exported to Sweden as SE-CMB. Its current status is not known. (*Rod Brown*)

Varsity T.1 WL628/U of the Central Navigation and Control School (CNCS) based at RAF Shawbury, photographed while visiting Blackbushe in September 1955. The CNCS was the RAF training school for Air Traffic Controllers. (*Rod Brown*)

Flying Training Command (1956–68)

A pair of RAF Training Command's jet training aircraft of the 1960s, resplendent in their silver and dayglo colour scheme of the period. Nearest the camera is Gnat T.1 XM709/95 with Jet Provost T.4 XP573/49 on its starboard side. Both aircraft also carry the badge of the Central Flying School then resident at RAF Little Rissington. (*Crown Copyright/Air Historical Branch image T-3019*)

The ten years following the end of the Second World War had seen a significant reduction in the number of pilots required by the RAF, which led to a major cull of training units. Some increase was again seen in 1950, at the beginning of the Korean War, although at this time only six Flying Training Schools existed.

By the end of the Korean War in 1953, the Piston Provost had joined Flying Training Command to begin a new era of Provost/Harvard training.

However, with new operational jet aircraft on the horizon – including the Canberra, Javelin, Hunter, Victor and Lightning – many in the service felt the piston-powered training aircraft were completely unsuitable as training platforms for future fast jet pilots. Shortly afterwards, when the Vampire T.11 joined Flying Training Command, it brought the Provost/Vampire training programme into being, which, while not being perfect, was at least a step in the right direction. However, the introduction of the Meteor T.7 alongside the Vampire T.11 gave some further impetus, although both aircraft were more suited to advanced jet training, especially the Meteor T.7, which suffered from a condition known as the 'Phantom Dive', which made the aircraft rather unsuitable for any form of basic jet training.

Thankfully, the Jet Provost T.1 and later a single T.2 variant, XD694, were designed to examine the possibility of all-through jet training and were soon undergoing trials as to their suitability for the role. While the Jet Provost T.1 and T.2 did prove the viability of the new training concept, the type did not demonstrate its suitability to accomplish the task and no further orders for either variant were forthcoming.

Thankfully, development work on the Jet Provost T.3 by BAC (having taken over Hunting Aircraft in 1960) was making good progress and the latter would eventually become the RAF's basic jet training platform and with it, the all-through jet training programme became a reality. Interestingly, the RAF was the first air force anywhere in the world to introduce such a programme, but other air forces would soon follow their lead.

Jet Provost T.3

Early in 1957 it was announced that the Jet Provost T.3 would be standardised throughout Flying Training Command in the improved T.3 version. The new variant differed from the earlier T.1 in having a more powerful Armstrong Siddeley Viper engine of 1,750-lb thrust, a shortened undercarriage, wing-tip fuel tanks, a clear vision canopy and a Martin-Baker ejection seat. Other improvements to radio and navigation equipment included the Rebecca Mk 8 DME (distance measuring equipment) and UHF instead of VHF radios. The first T.3 (XM346) made its first flight on 22 June 1958 and orders were placed for 201 aircraft. The type had a top speed of around 350 knots and could climb (eventually) to 25,000 feet, but was unpressurised and had a 1940s-style oxygen system installed. Despite its unspectacular performance, it was ideally suited to basic flying training.

The first Jet Provost T.3s entered service with 2 FTS at Syerston in June 1959, while the first course for *ab initio* students began on 7 October 1959 and ended on 22 June 1960.

In addition to equipping all the Flying Training Schools, the JP T.3 also served with the RAF College, Cranwell, as well as the CFS at Little Rissington, where it soon became known as 'the constant thrust variable noise machine'.

In later years, seventy Jet Provost T.3 aircraft had a mid-life upgrade to its avionics and radio equipment and operated as the T.3A. The last of the T.3A aircraft remained in service with 1 FTS at Linton-on-Ouse until withdrawn in 1993.

Gnat T.1

The Folland series of small, light, high-performance jet aircraft began with the Midge fighter in August 1954 and continued with the private venture Gnat single-seat fighter in July 1955. An initial order was placed for six Gnat fighters for development flying, but the type failed to obtain any further orders from the RAF.

In 1957, the Gnat's potential as a two-seat advanced trainer were realised and an initial order was placed for fourteen pre-production aircraft. In February 1960, an order for an additional thirty aircraft was then placed, with another twenty in July 1961. In March 1962, a final contract brought the total order to 105 aircraft.

The Gnat trainer differed from the single-seat version with two seats in tandem located into a lengthened fuselage, an additional 40ft² of wing area, outboard ailerons, conventional flaps, and a larger tailplane and fin. It also featured additional internal fuel tanks located in the wings, a redesigned jet intake and a strengthened airframe able to meet the RAF's fatigue life requirement of ten years, or 5,000 flying hours.

The first Gnat T.1 flew on 31 August 1959 before entering service with the CFS at Little Rissington in February 1962, followed shortly afterwards with 4 FTS at RAF Valley.

In 1964, 4 FTS formed its own aerobatic team, known as the Yellowjacks, with Gnat T.1 aircraft painted in a special all-over yellow colour scheme. In 1965, the Yellowjacks were replaced by a team of CFS flying instructors who were to become world-famous as the Red Arrows.

However, despite its airshow success, it was not long before the apparent shortcomings of the Gnat T.1's became evident. Having been converted from a single-seat fighter, the two-seat tandem cockpit was too small for taller pilots; the aircraft suffered with a poor serviceability record; and its handling was often too demanding for many foreign student pilots trained by the RAF. Consequently, a squadron of both single- and two-seat Hunter aircraft was soon added to the strength of 4 FTS. This new squadron provided the same seventy-hour syllabus for overseas pilots as well as RAF pilots not comfortably fitting into the Gnat.

Jet Provost T.4

Following the Jet Provost T.3, development work continued with a new improved T.4 variant, with the first of this new variant entering service with Flying Training Schools in November 1961. A total of 185 Jet Provost T.4 aircraft were ordered by the RAF and served with numbers 1, 2, 3, 6 and 7 FTS, the CFS at Little Rissington, the College of Air Warfare at Manby, and the RAF College at Cranwell.

Externally, the T.4 was physically identical to the earlier T.3, although it featured a 40 per cent more powerful Viper 11 engine of 2,500-lb thrust, permitting an improved performance, with a maximum speed now closer to 400 knots and the capability to climb to 30,000 feet. Many of the new T.4 aircraft joined the same Flying Training Schools as the earlier T.3, where they operated in unison, with the T.3 being used for the earlier training sorties, before students moved onto the T.4 for advanced aerobatics, high- and low-level navigation training, and high-level formation training.

This new variant proved particularly popular with aerobatic formation display teams including The Macaws (College of Air Warfare), The Gins (1 FTS), The Lincolnshire Poachers (RAF College Cranwell), The Vipers (2 FTS), The Red Pelicans (CFS) and The Gemini Pair (3 FTS).

Dominie T.1

The Dominie T.1 was a military development of the successful de Havilland DH.125 business jet. It was the very first jet-powered navigation trainer designed specifically for such a role to enter RAF service. The prototype Dominie T.1 (XS709) made its first flight in December 1964 and a total of twenty were ordered for the RAF.

The first aircraft entered service with 1 ANS at Stradishall in December 1965, where it replaced the Meteor NF(T).14 in service. The first navigator students to train on the new type passed out in April 1966.

Internal cabin arrangements allowed for two pilots, a staff navigator, a supernumerary crew member and two pupils working at a transverse navigation station at the rear of the fuselage. The aircraft carried a comprehensive fit of navigation equipment including Decca Navigator, a radio compass, Doppler and a periscope sextant.

RAF Stradishall operated ten Dominie T.1 aircraft as 'high/fast' navigation training platforms, alongside eleven Varsity aircraft for 'low/slow' training. Students enjoyed forty-five hours of flying instruction spread over twenty-one sorties, half of them at night. Training flights in the Dominie T.1 usually took place at between 30,000 and 35,000 feet. In the final stages of their training, students undertook exercises to Malta or Gibraltar.

In 1987, Dominie T.1 aircraft were joined in service with 6 FTS at Finningley, operating alongside Jetstream T.1 aircraft.

Flying Training Command becomes Training Command

Having been created from the elements of Training Command back on 27 May 1940, it was announced on 1 June 1968 that RAF Flying Training Command would be absorbed into the newly established RAF Training Command, with its headquarters remaining at Shinfield Park, Reading. The Command Badge was changed, and the motto became *Terra Caeloque Docemus* ('We teach on Land and in the Air').

The Bristol Brigand T.5 remained in service with the RAF until March 1958, when 238 OCU based at RAF North Luffenham was finally disbanded. This image shows T.5 VS837/N in formation with a Meteor NF.14, WS752, of 85 Squadron during a training sortie. (*Crown Copyright/Air Historical Branch image PRB-1-9413*)

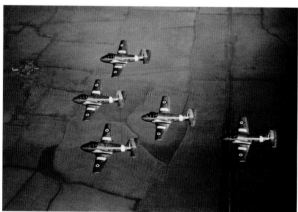

A neat formation of five Jet Provost T.1 aircraft of 2 FTS at RAF Hullavington, photographed on 12 March 1956. The five aircraft are XD676/Q-U, XD678/Q-N, XD680/Q-T, XD692/Q-W and XD693/Q-Z. (*Crown Copyright/Air Historical Branch image PRB-1-11416*)

From August 1955 trials were held at 2 FTS at RAF Hullavington to examine the concept of an all-jet training syllabus. Side-by-side courses were undertaken using both the Percival Provost T.1 (WV625/R-A pictured) and Jet Provost T.1 (XD693/Q-Z pictured). The trials were successful and the first students to undertake the new all-jet syllabus commenced their training at RAF Syerston in August 1959. (*Crown Copyright/ Air Historical Branch image PRB-1-11426*)

The sole military-registered example of the Percival Jet Provost T.2, XD694, photographed in 1957. This aircraft was the very last of ten development aircraft ordered in 1953 to validate the concept of jet-powered basic training aircraft modified to eradicate some of the issues found in the earlier Jet Provost T.1. It was fitted with shorter undercarriage legs, as well as a more powerful Viper engine within a redesigned rear fuselage. (*Crown Copyright/Air Historical Branch image PRB-1-13146*)

Early in 1957, it was announced that the BAC Jet Provost T.3 would be standardized throughout Flying Training Command. The first Jet Provost T.3, XM346, made its first flight on 22 June 1958 and was photographed while operating with the A&AEE at Boscombe Down in 5 April 1959. This was the first version of the Jet Provost to be widely issued to training establishments and entered service with 2 FTS at RAF Syerston in June 1959. (*Crown Copyright/Air Historical Branch image PRB-1-16475*)

The Air Cadets at No. 1 Gliding Centre, RAF Swanton Morley, operated several Slingsby T.21B Sedburgh TX.1 gliders including XN146, which was photographed during a sortie in March 1962. The Sedburgh TX.1 entered service in 1948 and a total of ninety-five were built for the RAF. The type was finally withdrawn from RAF service in the mid-1980s when they were replaced with the all-composite Viking T.1 gliders. (*Crown Copyright/Air Historical Branch image T-2996*)

Varsity T.1, WL670/A, of 5 FTS at RAF Oakington photographed in March 1962. The school had recently received the Varsity aircraft from 4 FTS at RAF Valley, which was then preparing to receive the new Gnat T.1 jet trainers. At RAF Oakington, the Varsity aircraft were used by 5 FTS to train crews destined for multi-engine aircraft. (*Crown Copyright/Air Historical Branch image T-3037*)

Sixteen Vickers Valleta T.4 aircraft were converted from earlier Valetta T.3 transport variants and initially entered service with 228 OCU at RAF Leeming. Its long radar nose distinguished it from other Valeeta variants, although there were many changes within its internal equipment. Others entered service with 2 ANS at RAF Thorney Island where WG256 was photographed in October 1962. (*Crown Copyright/Air Historical Branch image PRB-1-23958*)

Three Meteor NF.14 aircraft (WS744, WS774 and WS726) of No. 2 Air Navigation School (2 ANS) at RAF Hullavington were photographed in flight in 1962. The school remained in existence until 26 August 1970, when its functions were absorbed into 6 Flying Training School (6 FTS) at RAF Finningley. (*Crown Copyright/Air Historical Branch image T-3475*)

The Jet Provost T.4 made its first flight on 15 July 1960 and soon entered service with the Flying Training Schools. These Jet Provost T.4 aircraft (XP547/82, XP560/75 and XP566/81) operated with the RAF College at Cranwell and were photographed in 1964. (*Crown Copyright/Air Historical Branch image T-4419*)

The five distinctive yellow Gnat T.1 aircraft from the No. 4 Flying Training School (4 FTS) Yellowjacks display team photographed during a display practice from their base at RAF Valley in 1964. The team was the forerunner to the Red Arrows, which was formed the following year at RAF Fairford. (*Crown Copyright/Air Historical Branch image T-4720*)

The Dominie T.1 was a military derivative of the de Havilland DH.125 executive jet. The prototype of the military variant, XS709 seen above, made its first flight in December 1964 and twenty were built for the RAF. It initially entered service with No. 1 Air Navigation School (1 ANS) at RAF Stradishall in December 1965, where the first navigators to win their wings on the type passed out in April 1966. (*Crown Copyright/Air Historical Branch image PRB-1-29788*)

Three aircraft of 1 ANS, based at RAF Stradishall, were photographed together in 1965. From front to back: Dominie T.1, XS712/A, Varsity T.1, WF372/A, and an unidentified Meteor NF.14. All three types were used at the school for navigation training. The Dominie replaced the Meteor NF.14 as the 'high/fast' navigator trainer while the Varsity filled the role for 'low/slow' aircraft. (*Crown Copyright/Air Historical Branch image T-5965*)

The RAF acquired a quantity of Westland Bell Sioux HT.2 helicopters as training helicopters for use with the CFS (Helicopters) at RAF Ternhill where they replaced the Sycamore in service. This image depicts XV310/H, which remained in service with the CFS(H) until it was written off following a collision with an Army Air Corps Sioux helicopter in 1970. (*Crown Copyright/Air Historical Branch image T-7627*)

The Whirlwind HAR.10 differed from all earlier variants of the Whirlwind in RAF service as it employed a turbine engine in place of the original piston powerplant. The HAR.10 entered RAF service in January 1962 and with Flying Training Command shortly afterwards. Here, two Whirlwind HAR.10 helicopters (XP345/R and XP405/D) of the Rotary Wing of the Central Flying School were photographed while taking part in a survival exercise and although the location and identity of those being rescued is not clear, the images were taken during a survival course at RAF Gaydon, the home at that time of 2 Air Navigation School. (*Crown Copyright/Air Historical Branch image TN-1-3668*)

The Final Years of Training Command (1968–77)

The RAF's newest jet training aircraft, the Hawk T.1, made its first public appearance during its official roll-out at Dunsfold Aerodrome on 12 August 1974, where it was displayed with the aircraft it was planned to replace in RAF service – the Hunter T.7, Jet Provost and Gnat T.1. (*Crown Copyright/Air Historical Branch image TN-1-6978-15*)

By the time of the name change to RAF Training Command on 1 June 1968, the RAF was becoming a much smaller force, with a consequential reduction in the need for new pilots. That said, the RAF entered the 1970s as the third strongest nuclear power (in terms of the number of warheads), with the largest stock of nuclear weapons outside of the United States and Soviet Union.

The emphasis of the RAF was changing from that of a global role to a European one. The economics of the time, prompted by the 1970 financial crisis and devaluation of the pound, made the defence of Europe Britain's primary commitment. In 1971, the Labour government decided on the withdrawal of virtually all forces east of Suez by the end of the year.

Despite the tough economic conditions, RAF Training Command's re-equipment programme was underway by October 1973. The Chipmunk T.10 was being replaced by the Bulldog T.1, when deliveries to the CFS at Little Rissington began in April; the Jetstream T.1 was being delivered to 5 FTS at Oakington where it began replacing the Varsity T.1; and the Gazelle was introduced into Training Command at RAF Ternhill for helicopter training.

It was not all good news, though. Shortcomings with a lack of pressurisation systems in both the Jet Provost T.3 and T.4 fleet were exposing pilots to the risk of decompression sickness. Thankfully, BAC offered an upgraded design that became the Jet Provost T.5, with deliveries of a new, pressurised version beginning in 1969.

This was followed by the Jetstream fiasco. The RAF selected the Astazou turboprop-powered Jetstream to replace the ageing Varsity T.1 in the multi-engine training role, with twenty-six aircraft being ordered for the task. Deliveries began in 1973 to 5 FTS at Oakington. The Jetstream's entry into service was initially dogged by engine problems before the mid-1970s Defence Review drastically reduced the RAF's transport fleet to meet the new European, rather than global, emphasis. This saw the withdrawal of most of the RAF's fleet of long-range transport aircraft including the Comet, Britannia, and Belfast; in turn leading to a surplus of multi-engine pilots with nothing to fly. Consequently, multi-engine training at 5 FTS ceased and the new Jetstream aircraft were placed into storage at St Athan.

Jet Provost T.5

The RAF had already ordered 201 examples of the Jet Provost T.3 and a further 185 examples of the upgraded T.4 version, but both aircraft suffered several shortcomings that required improvement. The primary problem with both variants was the lack of pressurisation. With the increasing need for training at high altitude, both marks were regularly operating at altitude using only a basic oxygen system, exposing its pilots to the risks of decompression sickness in the event of a system failure, causing concerns among many Service aero-medical specialists.

To counter this problem, BAC offered the RAF a new design: the BAC 145, effectively a redesigned and improved Jet Provost featuring a pressurised cabin and designated the T.5. The new aircraft featured an automatically controlled pressurisation system, which began to operate at 8,000 feet. The aircraft differed externally from its predecessors in having a redesigned front fuselage, 14 inches longer, and which incorporated a larger clear-screen and pressurised canopy. The tip tanks from the earlier T.4 version were removed and replaced with two additional wing tanks, providing an additional capacity of 252 gallons. Initially, the design could have added wing tip tanks increasing fuel capacity by a further 96 gallons, but during flight testing the aircraft exhibited undesirable spin characteristics when flown solo.

The JP T.5 was fitted with a 2,500-lb thrust Viper 201 turbojet, as used in the earlier T.4. However, the pressurisation equipment and extra fuel capacity resulted in the T.5 being 1,000-lb heavier than the T.4.

With the closure of BAC's former Percival hanger at Luton in 1966, production of the T.5 was transferred north to the BAC factory at Warton. The prototype T.5 was a converted T.4, XW230, and made its first flight at Warton on 28 February 1967. A total of 110 aircraft were ordered by the RAF, with the first (XW287) being delivered to the CFS at Little Rissington on 3 September 1969.

Later, in a similar fashion to the T.4 avionics upgrade programme, ninety-three of the T.5 aircraft were upgraded to T.5A specification between 1973 and 1976 – now equipped with modern VOR, ILS and DME navigation equipment.

Last CAAC Unit Disbanded

During 1951, five Civilian Anti-aircraft Co-operation Units (CAACU) were formed to provide training for radar operators, as well as artillery tow targets for both the Army and RAF. As the name suggests, all were run by civilian organisations and manned by mainly former RAF pilots and groundcrew.

No. 3 CAACU was formed at Exeter Airport in March 1951 to take over the operations of the No. 17 (AAC) Squadron at Chivenor, and provided target facilities for guns right across the West

Country. In August 1954, it was combined with No. 4 CAACU at Llandow and became No. 3/4 CAACU, still operating from Exeter.

Throughout the lives of all five CAACU units they operated as part of Groups within RAF Flying Training Command, or later RAF Training Command, with a range of interesting aircraft including Beaufighter TT.10, Mosquito TT.35, Spitfire LF.16E and F.21, Vampire FB.5, Meteor TT.20, Meteor T.7 and Vampire T.11 aircraft. The primary role of the Vampire T.11 was the training or retraining of radar operators by providing practice intercepts (PIs) on a variety of ground equipment.

On 31 December 1971, the very last of the CAACUs was disbanded when 3/4 CAACU ceased operations at Exeter Airport. At the time it had been operating Meteor T.7 and Vampire T.11 aircraft to conduct its operations and to mark the occasion, a special formation was flown on 13 December 1971, led by a single Meteor T.7 (WA669/27) with three Vampire T.11 aircraft (WZ160/60, XH304/71, and XK624/32) completing the box. It was the last time that three Vampire aircraft would be seen flying together in formation.

The duties of 3/4 CAACU were later taken over by 7 Squadron at RAF St Mawgan, operating Canberra TT.18 aircraft.

Scottish Aviation Bulldog

The original Bulldog was designed and built by the ill-fated Beagle Aircraft Ltd and made its maiden flight at Shoreham on 19 May 1969. With the financial failure of Beagle Aircraft, Scottish Aviation acquired the project and set-up a production line at Prestwick, primarily to build aircraft for export to Sweden, Kenya, and Malaya. However, in 1972, the company received an order from the RAF for a total of 130 aircraft as their standard primary training aircraft to replace the venerable Chipmunk.

The first Bulldog T.1 for the RAF (XX513) made its first flight from Prestwick on 30 January 1973. The first two aircraft delivered (XX516/41 and XX515/40) arrived with the Central Flying School at RAF Little Rissington on 12 April 1973. This was followed by deliveries to 2 FTS at Church Fenton in June 1973, followed by the London UAS at RAF Abingdon in December 1973. Deliveries were subsequently made to all sixteen of the UAS operations where they replaced Chipmunk T.10 aircraft in service.

From the middle of 1974, a pair of Bulldog T.1 aircraft from 2 FTS became the RAF's only piston-powered aerobatic display team when The Bulldogs replaced the Chipmunk aerobatic team known as the Blue Chips.

Hawk T.1 and the Red Arrows

Hawker Siddeley, with its vast experience of designing and building military training aircraft, emerged from the MoD's competition in October 1971 as the successful bidder in a competition for an aircraft to replace both the Gnat T.1 and Hunter T.7, as well as some roles provided by the Jet Provost, in a planned major rationalisation of the RAF's training programme. The project was initially referred to as 'HS.1182' and later as the Hawk T.1.

An order for 175 aircraft was placed in April 1972 but there were to be no prototypes or pre-production aircraft. Instead, it was planned that five of the six aircraft used in the flight development programme would be refurbished and later delivered to the RAF as part of the production order.

The first production Hawk T.1 (XX154) was rolled out at Dunsfold on 12 August 1974 and made its first public appearance at a media launch. XX154 later made its first flight from Dunsfold on 21 August 1974 and subsequently appeared at the SBAC Show at Farnborough the following month. The Hawk was manufactured at three Hawker Siddeley factories: Kingston being the main design and production centre; Brough, which produced the wing, tailplane, and fin; and Hamble, where the rear and rear-centre fuselage units, nose cone, canopy and windscreen were produced.

The RAF took delivery of its first two Hawk T.1 aircraft at RAF Valley on 4 November 1976 when it replaced Gnat T.1 aircraft at 4 FTS. Interestingly, its arrival at Valley also spelled the end of the Hunter aircraft at 4 FTS as the ten hours of advanced training and weapons training previously flown on the Hunter, could be completed on the Hawk.

From November 1979, the Hawk T.1 also replaced the Gnat aircraft with the Red Arrows aerobatic display team, when the team's first of nine specially painted Hawk T.1 aircraft (XX266) was delivered during a ceremony at Bitteswell. The team went on to make its first appearance with the new mount in April 1980.

Varsity Withdrawn amid Jetstream Saga

Originally designed and manufactured by Handley Page at Radlett, the Jetstream project was acquired by Scottish Aviation at Prestwick in 1972, after Handley Page entered administration on 8 August 1969. The RAF had been looking for a suitable replacement for its fleet of ageing Varsity T.1 aircraft used in the multi-engine pilot training role.

In 1972, the RAF placed an order for twenty-six Jetstream T.1, with the first 'new' RAF aircraft (XX475) making its maiden flight at Prestwick on 13 April 1973. However, the first seven aircraft in the contract (XX475 to XX482) were not new airframes, as they had previously been built by Handley Page before it entered administration. Furthermore, the next fourteen aircraft (XX482 to 493 and XX496 to 497) were built by Scottish Aviation using unfinished Handley Page fuselages. Only the final five aircraft were manufactured new at Prestwick.

RAF Jetstream aircraft began deliveries to 5 FTS at Oakington on 26 June 1973, where they provided eighty hours of instructional flying for pilots in the multi-engine stream, replacing the Varsity T.1 in that role. Unfortunately, the mid-1970s Defence Review drastically reduced the requirement for pilots in the multi-engine training stream. As a result, the Jetstream's new role became temporarily redundant and all twenty-six Jetstream T.1 aircraft placed into storage at St Athan, pending a decision of their future.

Fourteen of these aircraft were later converted to T.2 specification as Observer trainers and transferred to the Royal Navy, the first of which (XX480) was delivered on 21 October 1978.

A decision was later taken to bring eight of the remaining twelve aircraft out of storage and deliver them to 3 FTS at RAF Leeming. The first aircraft removed from storage was XX497, which was reactivated on 25 November 1976 and delivered to its new unit in early 1977. All the reactivated aircraft were later transferred to 6 FTS at Finningley.

2 FTS moves to Shawbury

On 1 March 1976, No. 2 (Advanced) Flying Training School re-formed at RAF Ternhill to provide advanced helicopter training, conversion, and refresher courses. This was somewhat short-lived as, on 8 October 1976, they moved to RAF Shawbury as No. 2 Flying Training School (2 FTS), taking over command of the Central Air Traffic Control School in the process.

At the time of the transfer, 2 FTS operated an interesting mixed fleet of Wessex HC.5C, Whirlwind HAR.10, along with Gazelle HT.2 and HT.3 helicopters.

The End of Training Command

With the continued economic pressures on the Defence Budget, it was announced on 13 June 1977 that RAF Training Command would be absorbed into RAF Support Command. The continued downsizing pressures had continued and the need for a specialist command responsible for flying and ground training was felt to be unnecessary.

RAF Flying Training Command and Training Command had served the country from 1 May 1936 to 13 June 1977. During those forty-one years, it had seen the country through the Second World War, when it provided a constant flow of suitably qualified air and ground crew required to defend the country at its time in need. Since the Second World War, it has witnessed a wealth of changes – politically, economically, and technically – but always delivered its task.

The Jet Provost T.4 continued to serve Training Command and, in addition, became a popular mount for its various display teams. The College of Air Warfare at RAF Manby operated a four-ship team named The Macaws from 1965 until it was disbanded at the end of September 1973. This image was taken on 25 July 1970 and featured T.4 aircraft XS210, XS216, XP688 and XP680. (*Crown Copyright/Air Historical Branch image TN-1-6247-33*)

This Slingsby T-61A Falke motor glider was initially registered as G-AYUP before being transferred to military marks as XW983 in May 1971. It was evaluated as the first Venture motor glider for the Air Cadets at the various Volunteer Gliding Schools. Orders were later placed for a total of forty Venture T.2 motor gliders. (*Crown Copyright/ Air Historical Branch image PRB-2-1892-31*)

Resplendent in its Royal Air Force Training Command colours is Dominie T.1 XS731/J. In service with No. 6 Flying Training School (6 FTS) at RAF Finningley, it was photographed on 20 May 1971. (*Crown Copyright/Air Historical Branch image TN-1-6390-4*)

Varsity T.1 WF331/M from No. 5 Flying Training School (5 FTS) at RAF Oakington during a photographic sortie on 10 August 1971. In 1974, the Jetstream began to supersede Varsity aircraft and the type was finally withdrawn from Flying Training Schools in May 1976. (*Crown Copyright/Air Historical Branch image TN-1-6452-10*)

On 31 December 1971, the last of the Civilian Anti-aircraft Co-operation Units (CAACU) was disbanded. To mark the occasion, a formation was flown by members of the Central Flying School and 3/4 CAACU on 13 December 1971. The formation was led by Meteor T.7 WA669/27, with three Vampire T.11 aircraft (WZ616/60, XH304/71 and XK624/32) completing the box. It was the very last occasion that three Vampire aircraft would be seen flying in formation. (*Crown Copyright/Air Historical Branch image TN-1-6506-3*)

The prototype Jet Provost T.5 (a converted T.4, serial number XS230) made its first flight at Warton on 28 February 1968. A total of 110 Jet Provost T.5 aircraft were produced for the RAF, with the first being handed over to the Central Flying School at Little Rissington on 3 September 1969. Like its predecessors, the Jet Provost T.5 became a popular mount for the various jet formation display teams, including the 'Linton Blades' from No. 1 Flying Training School (1 FTS) at RAF Linton-on-Ouse, who were photographed during a wintry sortie in February 1973. (*Crown Copyright/Air Historical Branch image TN-1-6723-119*)

The first production Scottish Aviation Bulldog T.1, XX513, made its first flight at Prestwick on 30 January 1973. The Bulldog T.1 has been ordered by the RAF as a primary trainer to succeed the Chipmunk T.10 in service. A total of 130 aircraft were ordered and deliveries of the first aircraft were to the Central Flying School in April 1973. The first two aircraft (XX516/41 and XX515/40) arrived with the CFS at RAF Little Rissington on 12 April 1973 and shortly after their arrival, a special photographic sortie was flown. (*Crown Copyright/Air Historical Branch image TN-1-6749-45*)

Nine of the No. 4 Flying Training School (4 FTS) Hunter F.6 and T.7 aircraft, resplendent in their striking red and white colours, positioned on the ramp at RAF Valley on 31 July 1973. The aircraft are XG185/74, XF382/72, XF526/78, XF509/73, XG274/71 (all single-seat F.6 aircraft), XL567/84, XL696/90, XL609/80 and XL597/87 (all two-seat T.7 aircraft). (*Crown Copyright/Air Historical Branch image TN-1-6810-5*)

Jetstream T.1 XX476 photographed on 18 October 1973. XX473 was one of a batch of twenty-six Jetstream T.1 navigational training aircraft ordered from Scottish Aviation for use by the RAF. This aircraft had originally been built by Handley Page Ltd at Radlett as G-AXGL but following that company's liquidation was acquired by Scottish Aviation and reworked as XX476. (*Crown Copyright/Air Historical Branch image TN-1-6840-13*)

By 1973, RAF Training Command's re-equipment programme was in full swing. The Chipmunk T.10 was being replaced by the Bulldog T.1; the Jetstream T.1 was replacing the Varsity T.1; and the Gazelle was introduced for helicopter training. All three of the 'new' types were photographed while flying in formation on 18 October 1973 – no mean feat considering the disparate cruising speeds. (*Crown Copyright/Air Historical Branch image TN-1-6840-7*)

With the 100th Bulldog T.1 aircraft (XX672) having been delivered into service with No. 3 Flying Training School (3 FTS) at RAF Leeming on 16 April 1975, a number of special photographic formation flights were made to celebrate the event, including this one flown over the White Horse at Sutton Bank and featuring Bulldog T.1 XX519/1 leading a pair of Jet Provost T.4 aircraft (XR650/66 and XS219/60) from No. 1 Flying Training School (1 FTS) at RAF Linton-on-Ouse. (*Crown Copyright/Air Historical Branch image TN-1-7246-6*)

With deliveries of Bulldog T.1 aircraft now passing the 100-mark, the University Air Squadrons (UAS) were now starting to re-equip while relinquishing their old Chipmunk T.10 aircraft. One of the first to do so was the Cambridge UAS who flew four of their new aircraft (XX634/C, XX657/U, XX658/A and XX659/S) for a special photographic sortie on 24 June 1975. Note the tail code letters spelling out CUAS. (*Crown Copyright/Air Historical Branch image TN-1-7311-1*)

Having originally been ordered to replace the Varsity T.1 within No. 5 Flying Training School (5 FTS) at RAF Oakington from 1973, a change in the multi-engine policy found the Jetstream surplus to requirements and all twenty-six were placed into storage at RAF St Athan pending a decision on their future. During 1977, eight Jetstream T.1 aircraft were returned to operational status with No. 3 Flying Training School (3 FTS) at RAF Leeming. The first out of storage was XX497/4, which was reactivated on 25 November 1976 and was photographed shortly afterwards on 9 December. Later, all of these aircraft were transferred to No. 6 FTS at RAF Finningley. (*Crown Copyright/Air Historical Branch image TN-1-7636-9*)

No. 2 (Advanced Flying) Training School had re-formed at RAF Ternhill on 1 March 1976, to provide advanced helicopter training, conversion and refresher courses. On 8 October 1976, they moved to RAF Shawbury as No. 2 Flying Training School (2 FTS). This image depicts a formation of 2 FTS helicopters from RAF Shawbury in December 1977. From left to right are Wessex HC.5C XS485/A, Whirlwind HAR.10 XJ726/F and Gazelle HT.3 XW898/G. (*Crown Copyright/Air Historical Branch image TN-1-7806-2*)

On the same day,
Wessex HC.5C,
XS485/A, from 2 FTS
was photographed
while practicing
operating in and out
of small woodland
drop zones. (*Crown
Copyright/Air Historical
Branch image
TN-1-7803-4*)

No. 2 FTS Whirlwind
HAR.10, XJ726/F, was
undertaking similar
practice for the camera
on the same day.
(*Crown Copyright/Air
Historical Branch image
TN-1-7803-8*)

The first Hawk
delivered to the RAF
arrived at RAF Valley
on 11 November 1976
to join No. 4 Flying
Training School (4 FTS).
XX168 was one of the
earliest aircraft into
service with 4 FTS and
carries the badge of 4
FTS on the fin while
the last three digits
of the serial was also
used as the aircraft's
code. (*Keith Wilson/SFB
Photographic*)

Bibliography

Andrews, C. F., and Morgan, E. B., *Vickers Aircraft since 1908* (Putnam: 2nd edition, 1988).

Andrews, C. F., and Morgan, E. B., *Supermarine Aircraft since 1914* (Putnam: 3rd edition, 1989).

Bagshaw, Roy, Deacon, Ray, Pollock, Alan, and Thomas, Malcolm, *RAF Little Rissington – the Central Flying School Years 1946–1976* (Pen & Sword Aviation: 2006).

Barnes, C. H., *Handley Page Aircraft since 1907* (Putnam: 2nd edition, 1987).

Bowers, Peter M., *Curtiss Aircraft 1907–1947* (Putnam: 2nd edition, 1987.

Brew, Alec, *Boulton Paul Aircraft since 1915* (Putnam: 1st edition, 1993).

British Aviation Research Group, *British Military Aircraft Serials and Markings* (British Aviation Research Group: 2nd edition, 1983).

Bruce J. M., *The Aeroplanes of the Royal Flying Corps Military Wing* (Putnam: 2nd edition, 1992).

Fisher, M. D. N., Brown, R. W., and Rothermel, T., *Chipmunk – The First Fifty Years* (Air Britain (Historians) Ltd: 1996).

Flintham, Vic, and Thomas, Andrew, *Combat Codes – A full explanation and listing of British, Commonwealth and Allied Air Force unit codes since 1938* (2nd edition, 2003).

James, Derek N., *Westland Aircraft since 1915* (Putnam: 2nd edition, 1995).

Jefford, Wing Commander C. G. MBE, BA, RAF (Retd), *RAF Squadrons* (Airlife Publishing Ltd: 2nd edition, 2001).

Mason, Tim, *The Secret Years – Flight Testing at Boscombe Down 1939–45* (Crechy Publishing: 2nd edition, 2010)

Robertson, Bruce, *British Military Aircraft Serials 1878–1987* (Midland Counties Publications: 6th edition, 1987).

Sturtivant, Ray, *Flying Training and Support Units since 1912* (Air Britain (Historians) Ltd: 2007).

Sturtivant, Ray, *The History of Britain's Military Training Aircraft* (Haynes Publishing Group, 1987)

Tapper, Oliver, *Armstrong Whitworth Aircraft since 1913* (Putnam: 2nd edition, 1988).

Thetford, Owen, *Aircraft of the Royal Air Force since 1918* (Putnam: 8th edition, 1988).

Wilson, Keith, *RAF in Camera: 1950s* (Pen & Sword Aviation: 2015).

Wilson, Keith, *RAF in Camera: 1960s* (Pen & Sword Aviation: 2015).

Wilson, Keith, *RAF in Camera: 1970s* (Pen & Sword Aviation, 2017).

Wilson, Keith, *Royal Flying – A Pictorial History* (Amberley Publishing, 2017).

Documents

RAF Narratives: Aircrew Training (1934–42), Air Historical Branch.

RAF Narratives: Flying Training Volume II Organisation (1939–45), Part 1 Basic Training, Air Historical Branch.

RAF Narratives: Flying Training Volume II Organisation (1939–45), Part 2 Basic Training Overseas, Air Historical Branch.

Royal Air Force Air Power Review, Volume 19, Number 2, Autumn/Winter 2016, RAF Centre for Air Power Studies.

Royal Air Force Air Power Review, Volume 21, Number 2, Summer 2018, RAF Centre for Air Power Studies.